POCKET BOOK OF

knots

POCKET BOOK OF
knots

MARIA COSTANTINO

Published by SILVERDALE BOOKS
An imprint of Bookmart Ltd
Registered number 2372865
Trading as Bookmart Ltd
Desford Road
Enderby
Leicester LE9 5AD

© 2002 D&S Books

D&S Books
Cottage Meadow, Bocombe,
Parkham, Bideford
Devon, England
EX39 5PH

e-mail us at:-
enquiries.dspublishing@care4free.net

This edition printed 2002

ISBN 1–856056–31–7

Creative Director: Sarah King
Editor: Judith Millidge
Project editor: Clare Howarth-Maden
Photographer: Colin Bowling
Designer: Axis Design Editions Ltd

Printed in Singapore

1 3 5 7 9 10 8 6 4 2

CONTENTS

On knots

A flat Turk's head makes an attractive mat.

A monkey's fist is both decorative and functional.

Climbers prefer bulky knots designed to absorb strain.

Knots are as old as humankind: some 10,000 years ago, Neolithic people were using knots to tie their clothes and fasten their traps to catch food. In later civilisations across the world, knots and knotted cords were used as alphabets, calendars, calculators, tallies to record transactions and mnemonic devices to cue the memory. It was sailors, however, particularly those who served on the great sailing ships, who most fully developed the potential of knot-tying for both practical and decorative purposes. Long voyages left sailors with time on their hands, and, as most were illiterate, knotting (along with other crafts, such as scrimshaw) was the ideal way to pass the time. Under sail, these ships carried miles of rigging and there was always plenty of 'junk' — spoiled rope — to knot. The sailors gave the knots they devised descriptive names like the monkey's fist and the Turk's head, for example.

Each knot serves a different purpose and it is important to understand how different knots are best suited to the conditions in which they are to be used. One of the main reasons for selecting one knot rather than another is the relative strength of the knot. Knot strengths are of particular importance to climbers, who will favour bulky knots with several wrapping turns. These types of knot are designed to absorb strain and to avoid weakening the rope. Climbers routinely check their knots on a climb, especially when stiff, less flexible rope is used because it is more difficult to tie. Other factors that influence knot choice are the speed and ease of tying, the knot size and the reliability of the knot.

On knots

There are also different groups of knots:

stopper knots are also known as knob knots and are generally tied as a terminal knot in the end of a rope. Stopper knots are used to 'stop' the end of a length of rope, string or small stuff slipping through an eye, pulley block or hole. Stopper knots also prevent the ends of a rope from fraying and are used to weight the end of a length of rope to make it easier to throw. These types of knot can range from the simple to the elaborate: they include the knots that everyone has made to secure the ends of sewing thread and the decorative knob knots used to weight the ends of cords used for curtain tie-backs.

Hitches are used to tie a rope around an object like a pole, spar or ring. A line or rope is said to be 'made fast' rather than 'hitched' because only the knot itself is called a hitch. Some hitches work when the pull is at right angles, such as when a rope is made fast to a rail. Others will withstand a lengthways pull, as with making fast to rigging, masts and cables.

Stopper knots like the figure-of-eight prevent the ends of ropes from fraying or being pulled through holes.

Loops are knots formed when a closed bight is tied either in the end or in the central part of a rope. While it serves much the same purpose as a hitch, a loop is made to drop over an object, while a hitch is tied directly around an object and follows its shape. Consequently, hitches will undo or 'capsize' when removed from the object they are fastened to, while a loop can be used over and over again. Some loops are fixed into place, other loops are designed to slip and change size. These are called running knots and have nooses that tighten around objects when tied and slacken when the strain is reduced. Running knots must

A perfection loop is often used by campers to secure their tent pegs.

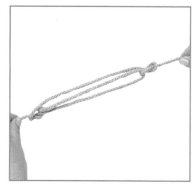

The sheepshank is probably the best-known shortening knot.

A sheet bend.

be among the oldest knots in the world: they were used by prehistoric humans to snare animals and also to make weapons.

Shortening knots are used to form nooses and loops and to shorten a length of rope instead of cutting the rope with a blade. The best-known shortening knot is the sheepshank (see page 105).

Binding knots serve two purposes: they can confine and constrict a single object or length of rope or they can be used to hold two or more objects or lengths of rope closely together.

Bends are a type of knot that ties two ropes together, or two parts of the same rope, usually in the ends. Its purpose is to form one longer piece of rope and ideally it should be possible to untie bends after use, particularly in valuable rope. However, in small stuff like string, a bend that is a permanent fixture may well be desirable when securely tying a parcel, for example. Where the material is only to be used once, the bend can be cut off and discarded. To ensure a secure bend, the ropes that are to be joined should be of the same diameter. Unusually, the sheet bend (page 79) is secure even when it is used to join different-sized ropes and is therefore a very useful knot.

On knots

Parts of a rope

The end of a rope that is actively involved in the knot-tying process is known as the 'working end'. (Anglers also call it the 'tag end'.) The remaining part of the rope is called the 'standing part'. At the end of the standing part of the rope — that is, the other end, away from the end you are working with — is the standing end. Rope that is folded back on itself without crossing over creates a 'bight'. You can create a bight to locate the exact centre of a piece of rope; when you have done this, you have 'middled' the rope.

When the two adjacent parts of a rope cross over a bight turns into a loop. A simple loop is an overhand loop. This is when the working end of the rope lies on top of the standing part. (An underhand loop is reversed: the working end lies underneath the standing part.) Add an extra twist to the loop and you will create an 'elbow'.

A 'turn' is when a rope passes around one side of an object or rope. A round turn is when the rope completes one-and-a-half circles around an object or a rope. Crossing turns are the basis of many knots. Doubling a knot gives it extra bulk, makes it more secure and also more decorative. Doubling simply means following the lay or route of the knot a second time with the rope, adding an extra circuit.

Parts of a rope

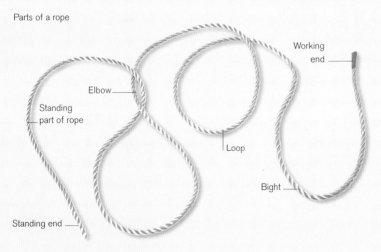

Working end

Elbow

Standing part of rope

Loop

Bight

Standing end

Ropes and cordage

Rope (left) is thicker than cord (right).

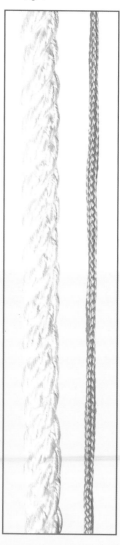

Rope can be made from either natural or artificial fibres that are twisted or braided and made in a variety of sizes. The size of rope is measured by its diameter, and the word 'rope' generally refers to a product that is over 10 mm (⅜ in) — although some specialised climbing ropes are only 9 mm (⅜ in) in diameter. Anything thinner than rope is called cord, twine or thread. Collectively, rope and cord are known as 'stuff', but when a length is used to do a particular job it becomes a 'line' — such as a heaving line, a life line, or even a washing line.

The properties of a rope, its strength, elasticity and durability, for example, are determined by the material from which it is made and by the way the rope has been constructed. Traditionally, rope was made by twisting fibres of natural materials together. The most commonly used materials were manila, sisal, coir, hemp, flax and cotton. The fibres were first twisted into yarn, then into strands and finally into rope in a process called 'laying up'. Look at an ordinary, three-strand rope and you will see how the strands go up and to the right, like a corkscrew. This is because it has been 'laid' right-handed. When the rope was made, the fibres were twisted to form a right-hand yarn. The yarn was then twisted in the opposite direction to form left-hand strands and finally these strands were twisted to form right-hand ropes. Uncoil one strand and see for yourself! Even with one strand uncoiled, the other two strands cling together, leaving a groove where the missing strand should be. This alternate twisting is what provides the tension to hold the rope together and gives it strength and flexibility.

Ropes and cordage

Sisal laid

Polyester braided sheath

Polypropylene laid

Elastic (bungee)

Climbing

Nylon laid

Climbing

Polyester

Jute braid

The problem with natural fibres is that they are only as long as the plant from which they are derived. The rough, 'hairy' feel and look of natural-fibre rope is caused by the ends of each individual fibre. These little hairs are useful in that they make ropes that aren't very slippery. On the other hand, natural-fibre ropes are not very elastic, they swell and become heavy when wet and, because they are natural, they will eventually rot and decay. In many activities, including sailing and climbing, natural-fibre ropes are used less frequently. Nevertheless, the beauty of the colours and textures, and the traditional appearance of natural-fibre ropes, still make them valued for their decorative features.

Natural rope.

Ropes and cordage

The development of man-made fibres has allowed the manufacture of ropes of superior strength. Synthetic fibres do not vary in thickness like natural fibres and they can be made in continuous lengths. Instead of twisting the fibres to make them cling, they can be 'glued' together in the manufacturing process. Artificial-fibre rope can be 'laid-up' like a natural-fibre rope or it can be braided with an outer sheath of 16 (or more) strands surrounding a central core (that is either braided, hollow fibre or made up of parallel or twisted filaments). Braided ropes — known by climbers as 'kernmantels' — are very strong yet also flexible.

On the whole, synthetic ropes are lighter, stronger and cheaper than their natural-fibre cousins. Nor do they rot, and they can be made resistant to chemicals, sunlight and salt water. They absorb less water, so their wet 'breaking strain' remains constant, and they are available in a range of colours. Nevertheless, knowing which type of rope to use is still important.

Nylon ropes are excellent for absorbing shock loads — they are good for towing and vital for bungee-jumping! Polyester rope does not stretch as much and, like nylon rope, it does not float. Polyester ropes are frequently used in sailing sheets (the ropes attached to sails) and halyards, but around the house you will also find polyester 'small stuff'. Polypropylene, while not as strong as nylon or polyester, is a good, inexpensive rope with the added advantage that it floats. This type of rope — often in bright blue or orange colours — is most

Synthetic rope.

Elasticated or 'bungee' rope.

Ropes and cordage

often used for water-ski tow ropes and for rescue lines, although because it floats it can foul a propeller. One big disadvantage of all artificial-fibre ropes is that they melt when heated. Even the friction of one rope against another can cause damage or weld knotted rope together, so it is vital that all ropes are checked regularly for signs of wear. Also, the smooth filaments of artificial fibres make for slippery ropes: knots can come undone and may have to be secured with specialised or additional knots.

There are many synthetic ropes on the market, some specifically developed for specialist use in different pursuits, such as climbing, sailing, angling or even for use around the home. Mariners should consult their chandlers or specialist rope suppliers about different ropes. Likewise, climbers should obtain specialist advice on the different properties of climbing ropes from specialist organisations and look for the label of approval from the UIAA (Union International des Associations d'Alpinisme).

CORDAGE CARE

There are few things more frustrating than a length of rope or cord left in a knotty mess. Ropes that have been maintained, cleaned and stored will last longer and be more reliable.

• Never leave rope lying around where it can cause a trip hazard. Coil it, secure it and store it well above floor level.

• When a knot is no longer needed, untie it. Leaving knots and kinks in rope weakens it.

• Keep rope and cordage clean. Wash off dirt or grit (which can cut and weaken fibres) and oil with warm water and washing-up liquid.

• Wash salt water from ropes used for water sports by soaking and rinsing them in fresh water before storing them. Make sure that all ropes (both natural and synthetic) are thoroughly dry before stowing them away.

• Inspect stored ropes at the beginning of the new season for wear or decay and replace them as necessary.

• Keep rope stored in a dry, dark, well-ventilated place. Strong sunlight will cause polypropylene ropes to decay, while dampness in natural-fibre ropes will cause them to rot.

• Synthetic cordage melts; some synthetic fibres also give off toxic fumes when burnt. Protect synthetic ropes from heat, fire hazards and any potential electrical sparks.

• Use the right rope for the right activity or job. Be aware of the breaking strains of ropes and that any knot tied in a rope will reduce this breaking strain.

Ropes and cordage

Storing rope

Not only is a coiled rope aesthetically pleasing, but coiling will also help to prevent the rope from fraying and acquiring kinks — deformities in the rope caused by over-tight loops which can damage and weaken the rope.

Alpine coil

This tidy method of coiling and securing rope is used by climbers and cavers. As well as keeping it neat for storage, it can be carried in a backpack, over the head and under one arm or as a split coil (with the arms passed through the splits).

1 Bring the two ends of the coil rope together to meet each other.

2 Bend back one end of the rope so that you make a bight about 20 cm (8 in) long.

3 Wrap the other end of the rope around the bight and coiled rope, trapping all of the parts.

4 Make a second turn around the coil and the bight, trapping the first turn securely.

5 Make a succession of turns, wrapping each tightly and snugly against the previous turn. Keep the turns neat and parallel.

6 Complete at least six wrapping turns and then tuck the working end through the bight and pull on the other end to secure the coil.

Ropes and cordage

Wrapped and reef-knotted coil

To ensure a completely tangle-free journey for any length of rope, this method of coiling and securing it is the best. A length of rope secured in this way makes the whole coil lie flat, making it ideal for storing in the boot of your car.

1 Bring the long ends of the coiled rope together. Tie a half-knot left over right and under.

2 Tie a second half-knot, this time going right over left and under.

3 Take the ends from the reef knot and wrap them around the coil in diagonal turns.

4 When the two ends meet opposite the reef knot, tie a half-knot left over right and under.

5 Add another half-knot, this time right over left and under, to make a second reef knot.

Fireman's coil

This is the simplest and quickest way of making and securing a coil of rope.

1 Bring the two ends of the coiled rope together.

2 Take one of the ends and make a small overhand loop.

3 Make a bight by passing the end through and then behind.

4 Tuck the bight through the loop from back to front. Pull it tight.

Ropes and cordage

Whipping rope

Whipping is a binding at the ends of a rope that prevents them from fraying. Whipping twines are sold by rope stockists; you should use natural-fibre twine for whipping natural-fibre ropes and synthetic twine for synthetic ropes. Once whipped, the ends of synthetic ropes should not be heat-sealed. An easy alternative to whipping is to use adhesive tape. Other methods of securing the ends of rope include using a proprietary whipping liquid; dipping the ends of small-diameter rope or thin lines into a latex-based glue; or fitting specialised plastic tubing over the ends of rope (the plastic shrinks into a tight seal around the end of the rope when the ends are held in the steam of a boiling kettle).

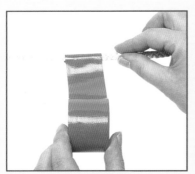

1 Wrap two turns of tape around the rope or cord where the cut in the rope is to be made.

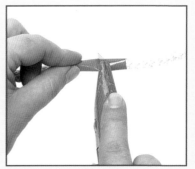

2 Using a sharp blade, cut down vertically through the middle of the taped portion. Try to avoid using broad sawing motions when cutting. This will minimise the fray and stop the tape from sliding around the rope. While it may not be as attractive as other forms of whipping, adhesive tape in different colours is useful since the ends of rope can be 'colour coded' to help you to remember which end or ends you are working with.

Ropes and cordage

Common whipping

In this easy-to-create whipping, the wrapping turns are made in the opposite direction to the lay of the rope. This counters the rope's natural tendency to unravel: as the rope ends start to unlay, they splay out, but are held securely against the whipping.

1 Make a long bight in the whipping twine and lay it alongside the end of the rope.

2 Wrap the working end of the whipping twine around the rope, trapping both legs of the bight with the first turn.

3 Continue to wrap tightly and evenly towards the end of the rope. Continue until the whipping is as long as the rope is wide.

4 Tuck the working end of the whipping twine through the remaining bit of the bight.

5 Pull the standing end to reduce the bight until it traps the working end under the whipping.

Glossary of terms

Bend The name given to knots that bind (bend) two separate ropes together.

Bight The slack part of rope between the two ends that is folded back on itself to form a narrow loop.

Blood knot A type of knot secured by numerous wrapping turns.

Body The bulky, tied part of a knot.

Braid Strands of rope plaited or braided together in a regular pattern. Generally, a braid is flat or two-dimensional.

Breaking strength The amount of load that a new rope will bear before it breaks. Breaking strength is reduced by wear and tear, by shock-loading and by knots.

Capsize What happens when a knot layout is distorted due to overloading or overtightening. It may also be done deliberately as a quick-release mechanism.

Cord Small stuff under 10 mm ($\frac{5}{12}$ in) in diameter.

Cordage The collective term for ropes of all sizes and types.

Core The inner part of a rope made from parallel, twisted or braided fibres.

Crossing turn A circle made by crossing the rope over itself.

Double Used as a verb: to double a knot. To follow the lead of a knot around again.

Elbow Two crossing points made by an extra twist in a loop.

Eye 1) A hole in a knot. **2)** The hole inside a circle of rope.

Frapping turns Additional turns made across lashing or whipping turns used to tighten previous layers of turns.

Half-hitch A circle of rope made around an object. The circle is kept in place by taking one end of the rope across and at right angles to the other end.

Heaving line The line attached to a mooring rope. It is thrown from a boat and used to haul the mooring rope in.

Hitch A knot used to make a line fast to an anchor point such as a rail, post, ring or other rope.

Karibiner A metal snap ring, often 'D'-shaped, with a pivoting gate that can be closed securely. These are used by climbers and cavers.

Kernmantel Climbing rope constructed from a core (kern) of parallel bunches of fibres contained within a tightly woven protective sheath (mantel).

Knot 1) The term for stoppers, loops and self-sufficient bindings (thereby excluding hitches and bends) **2)** The generic term for the tucks and ties made in cordage.

Lash/lashing To secure two or more adjacent or crossed poles with a binding of rope.

Glossary of terms

Lashing turn The turn used to bind poles together.

Lanyard A short length of cord used to lash, secure or suspend an object.

Lead (Pronounced 'leed'.) The direction of the working end as it goes around or through an object or knot.

Locking tuck The finishing lead of a working end that secures the knot in its finished form and without which the knot would unravel.

Loop A circle of rope formed by bringing two parts of rope together but without them crossing over each other.

Messenger The name given to a heaving or throwing line when it is used to haul or pull a thicker rope across an intervening space.

Middle, to middle To find the centre of a length of rope by bringing the two ends together.

Noose A loop which passes around its own standing part and draws tight when pulled.

Overhand loop A loop in which the working end is laid on top of the standing part.

Prusiking To climb a rope using knots that jam when downward pressure is applied but can slide up the rope when the weight is removed.

Racking turns Seizing and lashing turns made in a figure-of-eight fashion.

Rope Cordage over 10 mm ($\frac{5}{12}$ in) in diameter

Round turn A complete circle followed by a half-circle with part of a rope around an object.

Seizing Joining two ropes or parts of ropes together by binding them with twine.

Sling An endless rope or webbing 'strop' (pronounced 'strap').

Small stuff A general term for small-diameter 'stuff' like string.

Standing end The 'inactive' end of rope or cord.

Standing part The length of rope or cord that lies between the working and standing ends.

Tuck Passing one part of a rope underneath another part.

Turn Passing the rope around an object.

Underhand loop A loop in which the working end is laid beneath the standing part.

Whipping A binding used to prevent the ends of rope from fraying.

Working end The end of the rope used when tying a knot.

Basic knots

Everyone knows how to tie a simple knot, but most of us don't know what these knots are called or how they work. Some knots form basic stopper or knob knots in the end of a line (the type of knot you would tie in a piece of sewing thread to stop it being pulled through a needle). Others make simple loops or hitches — knots used to secure a rope to another object. The knots in this section are often the basis for the more complex knots that you will find in the following sections. Many elaborate knots start out as a simple overhand knot or a half-hitch. Once you know how to tie these, you can start to tie any one of the 4,000 or so different knots that have been devised and documented over time. Who knows, you may even end up inventing a brand new knot yourself.

Overhand knot (also known as thumb knot)

This knot is one of the simplest knots – so simple that everyone seems to know how to tie it! On its own, we use it as a simple stopper knot, such as when we tie off a piece of sewing thread to stop it from being pulled through the needle's eye. Yet the overhand knot is also one of the most widely used because it forms the basis for many more elaborate knots.

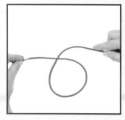 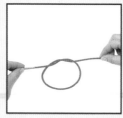 

1 Take the working end of the small stuff behind the standing part to make a crossing turn.

2 Tuck the working end through the loop you have formed.

3 Tighten the knot by pulling on the working end and the standing part.

Basic knots

Double overhand knot

Adding extra turns to a simple overhand knot will
produce a bulkier stopper knot.

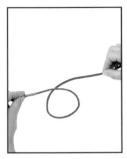

1 Take the working end
of the small stuff
behind the standing part
to make a crossing turn.

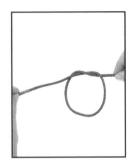

2 Tuck the working
end through the loop.

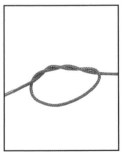

3 Tuck the working
end through the loop
a second time.

4 Pull both ends of the
rope tightly and push
your first turn into the
knot's centre.

Triple (and multiple) overhand knot
(also known as blood knot)

Knots with three or more tucks are collectively known as 'blood knots'. These very bulky stopper knots were used by monks and nuns to weight the belt cords that tied their habits at the waist. (It was said that the three tucks were a reminder of the Holy Trinity and of their sacred vows.) A more gruesome use for these knots was found by the British Royal Navy: until 1948, when the punishment was banned, multiple overhand knots were tied in the ends of the lashes of the dreaded 'cat o' nine tails' used for flogging sailors.

1 Follow steps 1 and 2 as for the double overhand knot (page 21). Then tuck the working end through the loop a third time. Remember to keep the loop slack.

2 Make a diagonal wrapping turn by pulling on both ends of the rope, twisting them in opposite directions.

3 Using your fingers, shape the knot to make all of the turns lie snugly together.

4 Pull on both ends of the rope to tighten the knot.

Basic knots

Two-strand overhand knot

This knot produces a very bulky stopper knot that can be used to tie together two ropes or cords that are lying parallel to each other. Unlike a bend, however, you can't pull the two parts of the rope in opposite directions.

1 Place the two ropes to be tied parallel to one another.

2 Tie a simple overhand knot.

3 Tighten the knot, taking care to keep the cords parallel.

Slipped overhand knot

This simple overhand knot has the added advantage of a drawloop that acts as a quick-release mechanism. The slipped overhand knot can also be untied as easily as it is tied.

3 Pull on the bight and the standing part to tighten the knot.

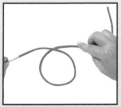

1 Take the working end behind the standing part to make a simple crossing turn.

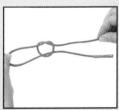

2 Form a bight by doubling the working end. Pass this bight through the crossing turn made in step 1.

Releasing the knot is easy – simply pull on the short working end.

Basic knots

Overhand loop

This knot is similar to the two-strand overhand knot, but with the added bonus of a handy loop. This is the knot that we all generally tie when we wrap up a parcel. And, as anyone who has ever received a packet tied in this way knows, the knot is pretty impossible to untie and has to be cut off!

1 Make a bight in one end of a cord.

2 Now form a loop in the bight you made.

3 Keeping all of the knot parts parallel, tie an overhand knot.

4 Pull on each of the four parts of the cord in turn to tighten.

Double overhand loop

This knot is bulkier, stronger and even more infuriating to untie than the overhand loop. (Again, it will have to be cut off after use.) Sometimes called a surgeon's end loop, it is also used by fishermen.

   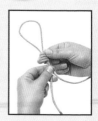

1 In the end of the rope, make a long bight.

2 Pass this bight twice through the crossing turn to form a double overhand knot.

3 Work the knot into shape by easing out any twisted knot parts and removing any slack.

4 Pulling on each of the four knot parts in turn, gradually tighten the knot.

Basic knots

Simple noose

Loops made in rope can either be 'fixed' knots or 'running' knots like this that slide so that the loop changes size. (Despite its simplicity, this noose can be dangerous! Never insert any body part – either your own or an animal's – into the loop.)

1 Using one hand, hold the working end of a length of cord.

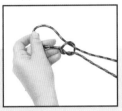

2 Tie a slipped overhand knot in the standing part of the cord (see page 23) with your other hand.

3 Pull on the loop to tighten the knot.

Half-hitch
(also known as single hitch)

Put under even the smallest strain, the half-hitch is possibly the world's most unreliable knot. It is nonetheless important as it forms the starting point of many more complex knots.

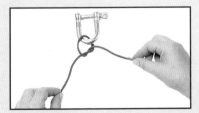

1 Tie an overhand knot around something firm, such as a curtain ring or broomstick.

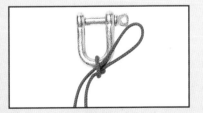

2 By leaving a slightly longer working end you can add a drawloop. Do this by not pulling the working end completely through.

CAMPING KNOTS

TODAY, A CAMPING HOLIDAY, WHETHER FOR A WEEKEND
OR FOR A MORE EXTENDED PERIOD, CAN BE AS
LUXURIOUS AS STAYING IN A RESORT HOTEL. HOWEVER,
MOST PEOPLE'S IDEAS OF CAMPING ARE OF NIGHTS
UNDER CANVAS, FOOD COOKED AND EATEN AL FRESCO
AND DAYS SPENT EXPLORING THE COUNTRYSIDE. A
CAMPING TRIP CAN BE A WELL-EARNED BREAK FROM THE
HUSTLE AND BUSTLE OF URBAN LIFE AND IT ALSO OFFERS
THE ADVENTUROUS MANY OPPORTUNITIES FOR WALKING,
CLIMBING, SAILING, CANOEING, FISHING AND, PERHAPS, A
LITTLE HORSE-TREKKING.
WITH THESE ACTIVITIES IN MIND, THE WELL-PREPARED
CAMPER WOULD BE WELL ADVISED TO CONSULT THE
SECTIONS ON FISHING, SAILING AND CLIMBING KNOTS,
SINCE MANY OF THE BENDS, HITCHES, LOOPS AND
BINDING KNOTS MENTIONED WILL ALSO SERVE THE
CAMPER. IN THIS CHAPTER, THERE IS A SELECTION OF
USEFUL KNOTS FOR TENSIONING TENT ROPES, FOR
SUSPENDING KNAPSACKS AND PROVISIONS OFF THE
GROUND AND FOR TETHERING HORSES. ALSO SHOWN IS
THE VERY EASY MIDSHIPMAN'S HITCH, A QUICK AND
SIMPLE KNOT FOR USE IN EMERGENCY RESCUES AND ONE
THAT EVERYONE SHOULD LEARN.

TYPE OF KNOT

LOOP

USE

SECURING ROPES TO PEGS

OTHER NAMES

NONE

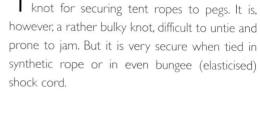

The perfection loop is a very useful camping knot for securing tent ropes to pegs. It is, however, a rather bulky knot, difficult to untie and prone to jam. But it is very secure when tied in synthetic rope or in even bungee (elasticised) shock cord.

1 Hold one end of a length of cord firmly. Make an overhand loop with the standing part.

2 Bring the short, working end over and lay it across the initial loop to make a pretzel-like shape.

3 Make a bight in the working end and pull it through the loop. Notice how you have just made a slipped overhand knot (an overhand knot with a drawloop; see page 23).

4 Take the short working end behind the long standing part of the cord.

5 Tuck the working end through the centre of the knot so that it is trapped beneath the two legs of the loop.

This ancient knot was originally used to string the bows used in archery. Later it was adapted by cowboys on their lassoes and was called a 'honda' knot (a corruption of the Spanish word for 'sling'). It's the stopper knot that governs the size of the loop, but, because this is tied in the working end, only limited adjustment is possible. It is a very useful knot for tensioning tent guy lines.

TYPE OF KNOT

LOOP

USE

TENSIONING GUY ROPES

OTHER NAMES

NONE

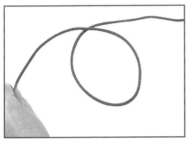

1 In the working end of the rope, make a clockwise underhand loop.

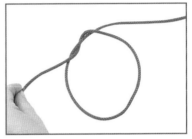

2 Make an overhand knot by passing the working end through the loop.

3 Going over the central part of rope and then under the outer part of the loop, take the working end through the topmost eye of the overhand knot.

4 Tighten the knot. To stop the rope pulling through, add a small stopper knot to the working end of the rope.

5 To adjust the size of the loop, simply adjust the position of the stopper knot.

Double overhand sliding loop

TYPE OF KNOT

LOOP

USE

ATTACHING OBJECTS

OTHER NAMES

NONE

This is an extremely useful knot for the campsite as it can be used to attach things to a cord to avoid misplacing them. It can also be useful around the home.

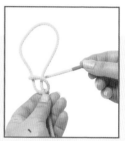

1 Make a crossing turn in the rope, ensuring that the working end lies underneath the standing part of the rope.

2 Next complete a turn by bringing the working end around the crossing turn.

3 To create a second turn, take the working end around the crossing turn once again.

4 Now insert the working end through the two turns.

5 Pull on the working end and the loop to tighten the knot. Adjust the size of the loop by pulling on the standing part of the rope.

This knot, tied in the bight, is also sometimes called an artillery loop because it was used to haul cannon and other artillery into position. Generally made in medium- or large-diameter rope, the loop of the man-harness knot is large enough to slip over the shoulder, leaving the hands free. This is a useful method for moving a trailer into position.

TYPE OF KNOT

LOOP

USE

MOVING HEAVY OBJECTS

OTHER NAMES

ARTILLERY LOOP

1 Make an anti-clockwise overhand loop in the rope.

2 Bring the upper section of cord around to the back of the loop.

3 Pass the right-hand leg of the loop underneath the middle standing rope part.

4 Then pass it over the left-hand leg of the loop, thereby making a small bight.

5 Hold on to the loop of the bight and pull the knot to tighten it.

Threaded figure-of-eight

This knot is basically a figure-of-eight loop, but tied in a way that will let you suspend a ring or other object, such as keys or a pocket knife, from the loop.

1 Leave a long working end in the rope and then tie a loose figure-of-eight knot.

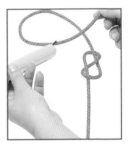

2 Thread the working end of the rope through the ring of the object to be suspended.

3 Tuck the working end into the uppermost crossing turn of the figure-of-eight from back to front, forming a loop around the ring.

4 With the working end, follow the path of the figure-of-eight. Keep the rope lying flat to the knot and don't let it cross over. (Note how you have now doubled the knot.)

5 Pull on the standing parts of the rope and work the knot into shape, making sure that the rope parts lie neat and parallel throughout the knot.

Three-part crown

This is a very secure knot, but after it has supported a heavy weight it becomes a little difficult to untie. A three-part crown is a good knot for safely hanging food or camping gear off the ground.

TYPE OF KNOT

LOOP

USE

SUSPENDING OBJECTS

OTHER NAMES

NONE

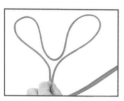

1 Make two equal side loops by folding down the bight in the rope. Hold the bight closed with one hand.

2 Make another loop below the two loops. The standing parts should lie on top of the right-hand loop.

3 Keep holding on to the base of the bight. Pick up the right-hand loop and turn it downwards to lie over the standing parts and bight base.

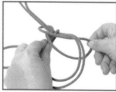

4 Hold on to the centre where all of the rope parts meet and take the top left-hand loop over the top of the middle left-hand loop and pass it through both parts of the lower loop.

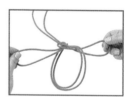

5 Pull on the left- and right-hand loops, making sure that both are equal. (If they are not equal in size, loosen the knot a little and pull gently on the smaller loop to adjust it.)

TYPE OF KNOT

LOOP

USE

GUY ROPES

OTHER NAMES

NONE

On the campsite, the midshipman's hitch is a very useful 'slide-and-grip' knot, which can be easily adjusted to tension guy lines.

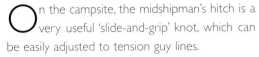

1 Make an overhand loop in the rope in a clockwise direction.

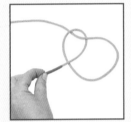

2 Bring the working end around and pass it through the loop you have just made.

3 Begin a wrapping turn by taking the working end up. This turn should cross and trap its own earlier turn.

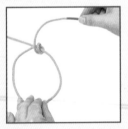

4 Bring the working end through the loop again so that this second turn lies above the first.

5 Bring the working end behind the standing part, outside the loop. Take it across the front of the standing part from left to right.

6 Around the standing part, make a half-hitch (page 25) and tighten it so that it lies alongside the other turns.

If you are unfortunate enough to need rescuing from a lake (perhaps after your canoe has capsized), a midshipman's hitch is the perfect way to secure yourself to a life line! Everyone, be they young or old, should learn to tie this valuable knot, the basis of which is the simple half-hitch.

TYPE OF KNOT

HITCH

USE

RESCUE

OTHER NAMES

NONE

1 Grab the end of the line that is thrown to you and quickly pass it between your legs.

2 Make a half-hitch around the standing part of the rope.

3 Jam a second turn on top of the half-hitch. In cases of extreme urgency, hold the working end very tightly with both hands, along with the standing part of the rope, and prepare to be hauled. If you have the opportunity, make another half-hitch on top of the knot you've made.

TYPE OF KNOT

HITCH

USE

SECURING ROPES TO OBJECTS

OTHER NAMES

LARK'S HEAD,
LANYARD HITCH

If you're lucky enough to be able to combine some horse-riding with your camping trip, then this simple hitch is useful for temporarily tethering your mount. It is one of the least secure of all hitches, however, as equal strain needs to be applied to both standing parts to ensure that the knot does not work loose. If your horse is very free-spirited, use a more secure method.

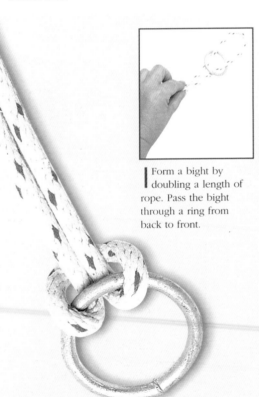

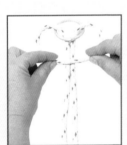

1 Form a bight by doubling a length of rope. Pass the bight through a ring from back to front.

2 Make the bight wider so that it extends to either side of the standing parts.

3 Pull the standing parts forward, through the bight, and pull tight.

Cow-hitch variant

This is an even stronger and more secure version of the cow hitch that can be used for tethering horses or even to suspend objects.

TYPE OF KNOT

HITCH

USE

SUSPENDING OBJECTS

OTHER NAMES

NONE

1 Take the working end of a line over the front and down the back of the anchor point or object.

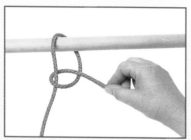

2 Make a single half-hitch with the working end of the line around the standing part.

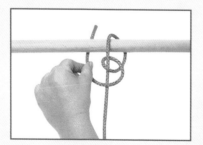

3 Take the working end across the front of the standing part and then up behind the anchor point.

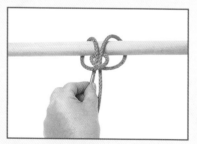

4 Bring the working end down, in front of the anchor point, and tuck it down through the turns so that it lies alongside the standing part.

This secure hitch is used to tether animals (even Lassie would have trouble slipping out of this one!) Use a long leash if you want to secure your dog so that it can sit or lie down.

1 Form a loop by taking the working end of the line through or around the anchor point to cross its own standing part of rope.

2 Pass the working end around and behind its own standing part and then out through the loop you've made.

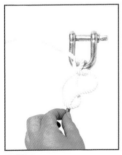

3 Form a running overhand knot with a drawloop by making a bight in the working end and tucking it through.

4 Tighten the knot and adjust the sliding loop, then secure it by tucking the working end through the drawloop.

This is very easy to tie and a very useful hitch. Tied on a bill hook or around the trunk and branch of a tree, it can be used to suspend a knapsack, tuck bag or any item that needs to be kept clear of the ground. The larger the diameter of the rope, the quicker it is to untie this hitch.

TYPE OF KNOT

HITCH

USE

SUSPENDING OBJECTS

OTHER NAMES

NONE

1 Pass the working end of the rope up behind the 'horizontal' part of the support.

2 Take the working end across, over the 'vertical' part of the support, around the back and then down, behind the 'horizontal' part of the support.

3 Bring the working end up, over the 'horizontal' part, and tuck it through the eye of the loop made around the 'vertical' part. Pull on the standing part of the rope to tighten the hitch.

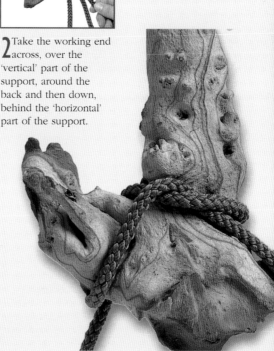

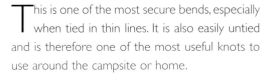

TYPE OF KNOT

BEND

USE

JOINING ROPES

OTHER NAMES

NONE

This is one of the most secure bends, especially when tied in thin lines. It is also easily untied and is therefore one of the most useful knots to use around the campsite or home.

1 Make a crossing turn in the end of a length of line so that the working end lies behind the standing part.

2 Make a crossing turn with the second line, passing the working end through the crossing turn of the first rope and laying the working end of the second line over the standing part of the first line.

3 Hold the two crossing turns together and pass both working ends up, through the two turns from front to back.

4 Pull on the working ends and the standing parts to start tightening the knot.

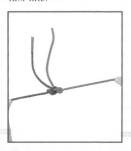

5 Separate the standing parts and then pull on each one to tighten the knot completely.

The advantage of this sheepshank over its 'ordinary' relative (page 105) is that it does not come undone. The two overhand knots that hold it together jam under strain and make it difficult to untie. It is, however, a very useful knot to know when a permanent shortening in a length of rope is required.

TYPE OF KNOT

BEND

USE

SHORTENING A ROPE

OTHER NAMES

NONE

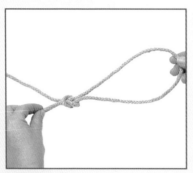

1 Make a simple noose (see page 25), leaving a long working end.

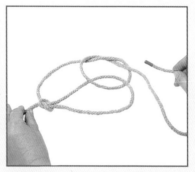

2 Double the working end back over to the right and tie an overhand knot in the end of the loop.

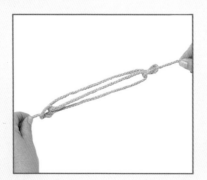

3 Tighten the knot by pulling on both ends of the rope.

SECTION

2

CLIMBING KNOTS

THE ROPE IS THE PRIMARY EQUIPMENT CARRIED BY THE CLIMBER AND IS USED FOR BELAYING, HOISTING, LOWERING AND RAPPELLING. THE FIRST CLIMBING ROPES WERE MADE OF NATURAL FIBRES, BUT THESE WERE NOT VERY STRONG. FURTHERMORE, NATURAL-FIBRE ROPES HAD LIMITED SHOCK-ABSORBING CAPABILITIES, WERE PRONE TO ROT, ABSORBED WATER AND BECAME UNMANAGEABLY STIFF WHEN FROZEN. AFTER WORLD WAR II, LIGHTWEIGHT, HIGH-TENSILE-STRENGTH NYLON, AND LATER POLYPROPYLENE, REPLACED NATURAL-FIBRE ROPES. THE STANDARDS FOR CLIMBING ROPES ARE SET BY THE UNION INTERNATIONAL DES ASSOCIATIONS D'ALPINISME (UIAA), WHOSE STANDARD FALL TEST IS AN 80 KG (176 LB) LOAD DROPPED 5 M (16 FT) ON A FREE FALL. UNLESS A ROPE HAS THE UIAA SEAL OF APPROVAL, IT MUST NEVER BE USED FOR CLIMBING. CLIMBING ROPES COME IN A VARIETY OF LENGTHS AND SIZES: 37 M (120 FT); 45 M (150 FT, THE MOST WIDELY USED); AND 50 M (165 FT). THE UIAA RECOMMENDS ROPE DIAMETERS OF 11 MM ($7/16$ IN) FOR SINGLE-ROPE CLIMBING AND 9 MM ($3/8$ IN) FOR DOUBLE-ROPE CLIMBING. SMALLER-DIAMETER ROPES, AVAILABLE IN 8 MM, 7 MM, 6 MM AND 5 MM, ARE USED FOR SLINGS AND PRUSIK LOOPS.

Alpine butterfly

TYPE OF KNOT

LOOP

USE

SUPPORT

Used as a middleman's tie-on, this is a symmetrical knot, tied in the bight, and used by mountaineers, who loop it around their chest.

1 At the point in the rope where the knot is required, lay a bight of rope over one hand.

2 Lead the working part of the rope around the hand a second time to complete one round turn.

3 Add a third turn around the hand.

4 Pick up, from the top of the hand, the turn nearest your palm and pass it over the next one so that it is now the middle turn.

5 Pick up the turn nearest your palm and pass it, towards your fingertips, over the two other turns.

6 Tuck the rope that is now on the left-hand side (nearest your fingertips) under the two other turns.

7 Pull out a bight the required size and tighten by pulling on both standing parts of the bights.

TYPE OF KNOT

LOOP

USE

SUPPORT

OTHER NAMES

FLEMISH LOOP, GUIDE KNOT

This knot is tied on a loop of rope and is used as the end tie in climbing. It is adjusted by feeding one strand of the rope through the knot and tightening afterwards. The great advantage of this knot is that it is easy to tie, but even if it is tied incorrectly it will still be quite safe as an overhand knot. However, when you tie a figure-of-eight on the bight, always check to make sure that the main rope lies outside the first bend in the knot.

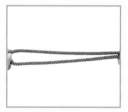

1 Make a long bight in the end of a length of cord or rope. If this is to go around your waist, make the size to fit.

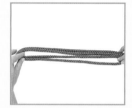

2 Fold the bight back on itself, making sure that you keep the rope parts neat and parallel.

3 Make two turns around the standing part. Keep all the rope parts parallel.

4 Pass the right-hand bight through the eye of the left.

5 Pull on the bight and the standing part to tighten the knot.

Frost knot

This climbing knot, devised by Tom Frost during the 1960s, is not usually tied in cord. Instead, climbers tie this simple overhand loop in webbing to create improvised climbing ladders called étriers (the French for 'stirrups'), which are clipped into pitons and bolts.

TYPE OF KNOT

LOOP

USE

SUPPORT

OTHER NAMES

NONE

1 At one end of a length of webbing, make a short bight.

2 Between the two flat sections of the bight, insert the other end.

3 With all three parts of the webbing, make a loose, anti-clockwise overhand loop.

4 Bring the bight around behind the loop, together with its extra end of webbing, and pull them through.

5 Tighten the knot, making sure that all three of the sections are lying flat.

2 Flemish bend

TYPE OF KNOT

LOOP

USE

SUPPORT, JOINING ROPES

OTHER NAMES

FIGURE-OF-EIGHT BEND

A simple knot to tie, the Flemish bend is also one of the strongest bends that you can tie in synthetic rope. It is well liked by climbers, and is a useful alternative to the single or double fisherman's knot (see page 64) for joining two ropes securely together.

1 Ensuring that the working end lies on top of the standing part, make a loop in one end of a length of rope.

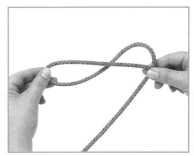

2 Hold the loop securely and give it a half-twist.

3 Make the figure-of-eight outline by tucking the working end through the loop above the twist.

4 Pick up the working end of the second length of rope and place it parallel to the first working end.

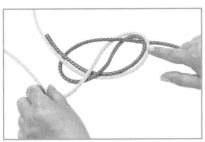

5 Keeping to the outside of the first bend, follow the lead of the first rope with the working end of the second rope.

6 Continuing to follow the lead around, transfer to the inside of the second bend.

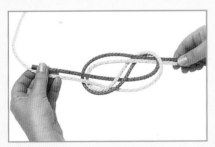

7 Pull on each working end and standing part in turn to tighten the knot.

2 Double figure-of-eight bend

TYPE OF KNOT

LOOP

USE

SHOCK-ABSORPTION

OTHER NAMES

NONE

At first glance, this knot looks rather like the fisherman's knot (see page 64). However, close inspection reveals that in the double figure-of-eight bend both sides are identical. When the two knots are a couple of inches apart, the double figures-of-eight will slide together, absorbing a sudden shock or jerk on the rope.

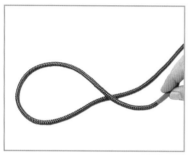

1 Ensuring that the working end lies on top of the standing part, make a loop in one end of a length of rope.

2 Hold the loop securely and give it a half-twist.

3 Make the figure-of-eight outline by tucking the working end through the loop above the twist.

4 Insert the working end of the second length of rope through the first knot.

5 Tie a second figure-of-eight knot in the second rope and around the first, a couple of inches down the standing part of the first rope.

6 Remove slack from the individual knot by pulling on the working ends of the rope.

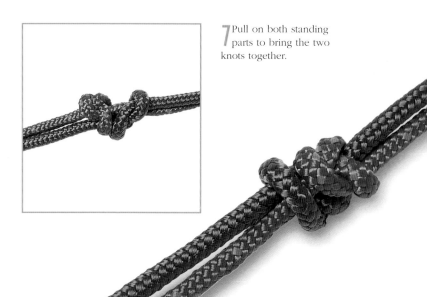

7 Pull on both standing parts to bring the two knots together.

This knot was created by Canadian climber Robert Chisnall. Shock-loading will cause it to slide until friction reduces the load to a point when it will hold. Pull on the standing part of the rope to test the knot.

1 With the working end lying over the standing part of the rope, make a loop.

2 With the working end, make two turns around the standing part of the rope.

3 Pass the working end around both legs of the loop.

4 Tuck the working end underneath the second wrapping turn.

5 Pull on the loop and the working end to tighten the knot.

Tarbuck knot

This knot relies for its grip on the dog's leg made in the standing part of the rope. Developed for climbers, the Tarbuck knot is used when the rope will be subject to heavy or sudden strain. It does not chafe the rope, but neither is it easy to undo.

TYPE OF KNOT

BEND

USE

TAKING STRAIN

OTHER NAMES

NONE

1 With the working end lying over the standing part of the rope, make a loop.

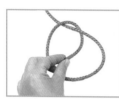

2 Tuck the working end down, through the loop you've just made.

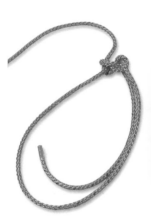

3 Start to make a second wrapping turn by taking the working end up, through the eye of the loop.

4 After completing two turns around the standing part of the rope, pass the working end behind the standing part of the rope.

5 Bring the working end around the front of the standing part and pass it, from right to left, through its latest loop.

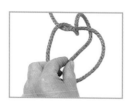

6 Gradually tighten the knot until all of the slack is removed.

TYPE OF KNOT

HITCH

USE

CONNECTING ROPE TO ANCHOR

OTHER NAMES

NONE

This knot is used for connecting a rope to an anchor point. It is useful because it is easy to release the rope when weighted. While the same thing could be achieved with a straightforward sling, it would be difficult, if not impossible, to unclip it under load, and it would probably have to be cut off with a knife.

1 Pass the working end of the loop through the karabiner from front to back.

2 Pass the loop through the karabiner again, keeping all of the rope parts parallel.

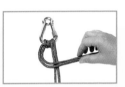

3 Bring the working end across the standing parts of the rope.

4 Take the working end around the standing parts three times, keeping the rope parts neat and parallel.

5 Make a long bight in the working end of the loop and pass it part way from back to front through the two legs of the standing part.

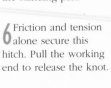

6 Friction and tension alone secure this hitch. Pull the working end to release the knot.

Klemheist knot

This is a variation on the Prusik knot, but is less likely to jam and easier to loosen. The sling is wound around the main rope in a spiral and then threaded through itself. The amount of friction can be controlled by increasing or decreasing the number of turns. The Klemheist knot can also be tied using 2.5 cm (1 in) tubular-nylon webbing on 11 mm (7⁄16 in) rope, and it will grip and slide like tensile cord. Check and test the knot for security before using it to take any strain.

TYPE OF KNOT

HITCH

USE

SLIDE AND GRIP

OTHER NAMES

NONE

1 Make a bight and lay it behind the main climbing rope.

2 Wrap the bight around the main rope. This should be in an upwards direction. Imagine that it is 'climbing up' and along the rope.

3 Continue to wrap the sling upwards. Ensure that both legs of the sling stay flat and parallel. Complete four or five turns around the main rope.

4 Tighten and neaten the turns. Bring the working bight down to the sling's standing part.

5 Tuck the standing tail of the sling through the working bight.

6 Pull downwards on the tail of the sling to lock the Klemheist knot firmly into position.

TYPE OF KNOT

HITCH

USE

SLIDE AND GRIP

OTHER NAMES

NONE

Named after Dr Carl Prusik, this is quite a simple knot to tie and is much used in climbing because it grips under load, but can be released and moved along the rope when unloaded. The Prusik knot is tied on a climbing rope using 5 mm, 6 mm or 7 mm tensile cord on half 9 mm or full rope of 11 mm. The knot must be kept symmetrical, with no overlapping of the windings, otherwise it could slip under load. Note, however, that the effectiveness of a Prusik knot will vary depending on the type of rope (sheath or laid), the type of Prusik cord (laid, sheath or kevlar), water content (it may also slip in wet or icy conditions), dirt and temperature. As with all climbing activities, practice in safe, controlled conditions cannot be overemphasised.

1 Open out a loop at one end of a sling and lay the loop on top of the main rope.

2 Bring the loop around and then behind the main rope.

3 Pass the sling's tail through the loop.

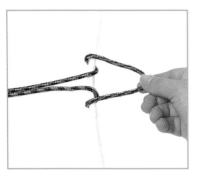

4 Take the loop around the main rope once again.

5 Using one hand, keep firm hold of the loop.

6 Pass the tail of the sling through the loop once again.

7 To tighten the knot, pull on the tail of the sling.

TYPE OF KNOT

HITCH

USE

PULLEY SYSTEMS

OTHER NAMES

NONE

This knot is useful in pulley systems, particularly when hoisting a casualty. The sling is clipped into a karabiner and wound around the main rope and the karabiner's back bar in a descending spiral. The friction can be controlled by the number of turns. Although it takes two hands to tie, the Bachmann knot is superior to the Prusik knot, particularly in wet or icy conditions. Note that when strain is applied, it is to the sling and *never* to the karabiner.

1 Clip a karabiner onto a sling. Hold the long side of the karabiner against the main rope, with the sling behind the main rope.

2 Wind the tail of the sling around the main rope and the long side of the karabiner to bind them loosely together.

3 Continue to bind the karabiner to the main rope along the long side and then bring the tail of the sling through the karabiner to the front of the knot.

4 Apply strain to the tail of the sling to tighten the knot.

5 To slide the knot along the main rope, release the strain on the tail of the sling and push the karabiner to move the knot along the rope. Apply strain to the tail of the sling to lock the knot.

Italian hitch

This is a versatile friction hitch for belaying live climbing rope in both direct or indirect belays and is the official means of belaying of the Union International des Associations d'Alpinisme. It gives enough dynamic friction to allow even the most serious of falls to be held with ease. A further design feature is that the hitch is reversible. Although it can be used for abseiling, this is not recommended because it results in kinked rope.

TYPE OF KNOT

HITCH

USE

BELAYING

OTHER NAMES

SLIDING-RING HITCH

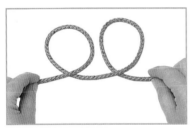

1 Make a pair of crossing turns so that the right strand of each turn lies on top of the left strand.

2 Fold the left-hand crossing turn over so that it lies on top of the right-hand crossing turn.

3 Pass the karabiner from right to left through the loops.

4 To slip the knot, apply strain to the left (loaded) rope. Control the amount and speed of slip by pulling on the right (braking) rope.

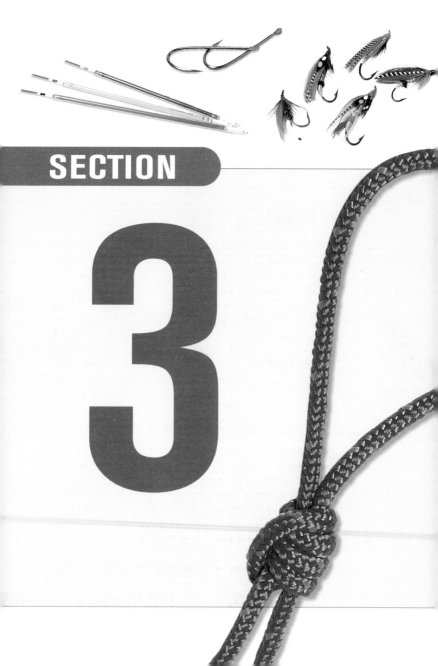

SECTION

3

FISHING KNOTS

ALL ANGLERS NEED TO KNOW HOW TO TIE KNOTS, MAINLY
BECAUSE THERE WILL USUALLY BE AT LEAST TWO KNOTS
IN A RIG. ONE KNOT WILL JOIN THE LINE TO THE REEL OR
POLE, ANOTHER WILL JOIN THE HOOK OR LURE TO THE
LINE. IN THE PAST, WHEN ANGLERS USED NATURAL LINES
OF SILK, COTTON OR FLAX WITH A SHORT GUT CAST, THEY
WOULD HAVE MOSTLY USED THE VERY SIMPLE CLOVE
HITCH. THIS IS QUITE A LOOSE KNOT, BUT WHEN IT IS PUT
UNDER STRAIN IT TIGHTENS UP AND BECOMES VERY
SECURE. WITH THE WIDESPREAD USE OF MODERN NYLON,
MONOFILAMENT AND BRAIDED LINES, WHICH ARE ELASTIC,
FLEXIBLE AND SLIPPERY, A LOOSE KNOT WILL SLIP AND
EVEN UNTIE AS SOON AS STRAIN IS PLACED ON IT.
ANGLERS HAVE THUS DEVELOPED A NUMBER OF KNOTS
AND LOOPS FOR ATTACHING HOOKS AND FOR BENDING
(JOINING) DIFFERENT THICKNESSES OF LINES. WHETHER
TIED IN NATURAL FIBRE OR IN NYLON LINE, A KNOT IS A
POTENTIAL WEAK POINT. DIFFERENT TYPES OF FISHING
REQUIRE A VARIETY OF KNOTS OF ASSORTED STRENGTHS.
IT IS ESSENTIAL TO CONSIDER THE DIFFERENCE BETWEEN
THE DRY BREAKING STRAIN OF THE LINE AS QUOTED BY
THE MANUFACTURER, AND THE ACTUAL WET BREAKING
STRAIN. ALLOW FOR AROUND **10** PER CENT LOSS.

3 Blood bight

TYPE OF KNOT

LOOP

USE

FLY FISHING

OTHER NAMES

NONE

This simple, four-stage knot is used to make loops in fly-fishing leaders. It's a little like the basic overhand loop (page 24), but this version produces a much more streamlined knot.

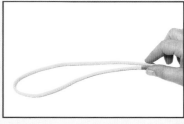

1 Make a long bight in the working end of the line.

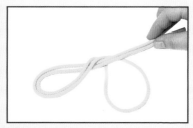

2 Double-back the bight and wrap it around the standing parts.

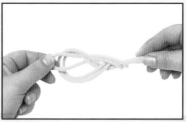

3 Pass the bight from back to front through the doubled loop.

4 Pull the knot tight and trim off the tag end.

Water knot

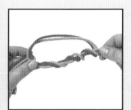

The water knot is a development of the double overhand loop. However, instead of forming the knot in the bight of the line to create a loop, the water knot is made on the married, shorter ends of two lines to be fastened. The water knot is an excellent choice for tying a leader containing one or more droppers.

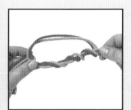

TYPE OF KNOT

BLEND

USE

TYING A LEADER

OTHER NAMES

NONE

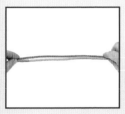

1 Lay the two lines parallel and close to one another, with the working ends of each facing in opposite directions and overlapping by about 15 cm (6 in).

2 Hold the two lines together and form them into a wide loop. Keep the lines neat and parallel to each other.

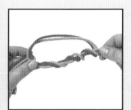

3 Keeping the two lines together, pass the ends through the loop four times. Again, keep the lines parallel.

4 Pull on the two lines to tighten the loop into a knot. Trim off the excess tag ends.

Fishing knots • **63**

3 Fisherman's knot

TYPE OF KNOT

LOOP

USE

JOINING TWO LINES

OTHER NAMES

ANGLER'S KNOT,
ENGLISHMAN'S KNOT,
HALIBUT KNOT

This is a very old knot, said to have been used by the ancient Greeks. The two overhand knots jam against each other when the standing parts of the two ropes are pulled. The short working ends lie in opposite directions, yet almost parallel to their standing parts, creating a very streamlined knot.

1 With the working ends of each line facing in opposite directions, lay the two lines parallel and close to each other.

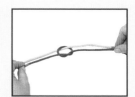

2 Tie an overhand knot around the upper line with the working end of the lower line.

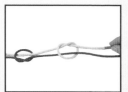

3 With the upper working end, tie an overhand knot around the lower line.

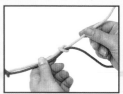

4 Pull on both working ends to tighten the individual knots.

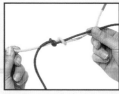

5 To untie and tighten the knots, pull on the standing parts.

Simple to tie, this is a particularly useful knot for attaching a thin line to a thicker one. Because it produces a secure knot, it has traditionally been used by cod fishermen on their trawl nets.

TYPE OF KNOT

HITCH

USE

JOINING LINES

OTHER NAMES

NONE

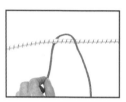

1 Pass the working end of the thinner line from front to back around the thicker line. Bring the working end left and forward of its own standing part.

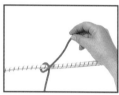

2 Take the working end up and diagonally across the front of both the standing part and the thicker line.

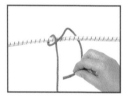

3 Pass the working end down, behind the thicker line, so that it emerges to the right and front of the standing part of the line.

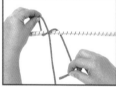

4 Create an upper bight by pulling up on the standing part.

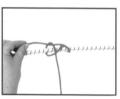

5 Tuck the working end through the bight.

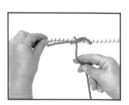

6 Trap the working end by pulling down on the standing part.

3 Albright special

TYPE OF KNOT

BEND

USE

JOINING LINES

OTHER NAMES

NONE

This is another angler's knot used to tie monofilaments to braid. It makes an attractive knot and is useful for securing together two lines of different diameters.

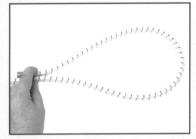

1 Make a bight in the working end of the larger-diameter line.

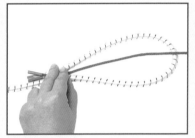

2 Bring the working end of the second, thinner line over and parallel to the initial bight. Hold the thinner line firmly against the bight.

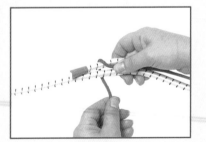

3 With your other hand, take the working end of the thinner line over one side of the bight and back behind both legs of the bight.

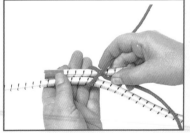

4 Take the working end of the thinner line back over the top of the bight, securely trapping its own standing part in the process.

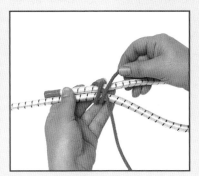 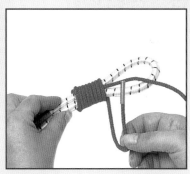

5 Take a second full turn neatly next to the first rope, making sure that its standing part is trapped at each turn.

6 Continue to wrap both legs of the bight with the working end of the thinner rope, making sure that its own standing part is trapped at each turn.

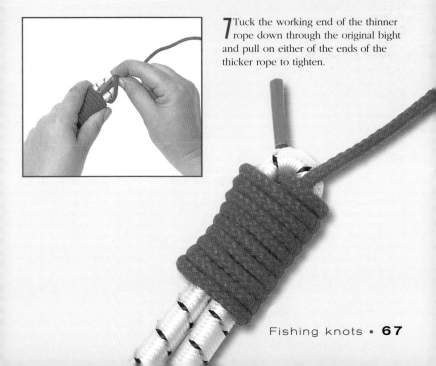

7 Tuck the working end of the thinner rope down through the original bight and pull on either of the ends of the thicker rope to tighten.

TYPE OF KNOT

HITCH

USE

JOINING LINES TO TACKLE

OTHER NAMES

NONE

This knot is used for attaching hooks, swivels and leads, especially when their wires are of a similar diameter to the line being used.

1 Thread the working end of the line through the eye of the hook, swivel or lead.

2 Next twist together the working and standing ends.

4 Push the turns up against the hook and then bring the working end up behind the standing part and tuck it down through the loop at the hook end.

3 Make four or five more twists, keeping the tension even.

5 Pull tight on the standing part to tighten the knot. Trim off the tag end.

Palomar knot

This very strong knot is said to be at least 95 per cent efficient! It is mostly used to attach a bight in a line to a swivel, sinker, hook or lure when there is likely to be a great deal of strain.

TYPE OF KNOT

HITCH

USE

JOINING LINES TO TACKLE

OTHER NAMES

NONE

1 Make a bight by doubling the end of a line. Pass this through the ring, front to back.

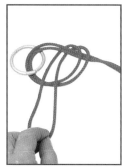

2 Tie an overhand knot by bringing the bight back across itself and tucking it through the loop formed.

3 Push the ring down through the bight.

4 Carefully work the bight all the way over the knot parts. Trim off the tag ends.

3 Jansik special

TYPE OF KNOT

HITCH

USE

JOINING LINES TO TACKLE

OTHER NAMES

NONE

This is another extremely strong and efficient hitch for a hook, line or swivel. The strength comes from the double-turn through the ring, coupled with the extra security of the triple-tucking of the tag end. At the same time, however, the Jansik special is a very compact knot.

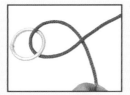

1 Take the working end of the line from back to front. Take it through the ring first and then under the standing part.

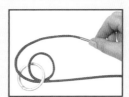

2 Create a round turn by taking the working end through the ring a second time.

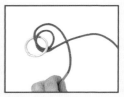

3 Pass the working end under the standing part of the line.

4 Make a wrapping turn by taking the working end over the two turns.

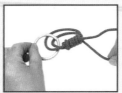

5 Now tuck the working end through the loop. Make a second wrapping turn, but wrap away from the ring.

6 After completing three or four turns, carefully tighten the knot by removing the slack.

Spade-end knot

This knot is used to tie monofilaments to spade-end (eyeless) hooks. Although spade-end hooks can be bought already tied to nylon, most anglers prefer to tie their own, as shop-bought versions seem to come untied just at that crucial moment! Here we demonstrate using a rope as the foundation object.

TYPE OF KNOT

HITCH

USE

JOINING LINES TO TACKLE

OTHER NAMES

SPADE-END WHIP

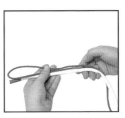

1 Make a loop in the line and arrange it so that the short end is alongside, and parallel to, the thicker line.

2 Keeping the short end in its position, wrap the body of the loop so that both parts of the loop are held, as well as the thicker line.

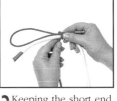

3 Continue to make tight wrapping turns, with each turn lying close to the preceding one. Complete seven wrapping turns.

4 Pass what remains of the working end through the bight.

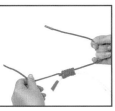

5 Remove the remaining slack in the bight by pulling the short end. Then pull on both ends in opposite directions to tighten the knot. Trim off the tag end.

③ Uni knot

TYPE OF KNOT

HITCH

USE

JOINING LINES TO TACKLE

OTHER NAMES

DORMHOF KNOT

This is one of the strongest knots used by anglers today. It's a very useful knot for connecting lead to a shock-leader. It is also popular with deep-sea anglers and when hooks are tied directly to reel lines.

1 Pass the working end of the line through the eye of the hook.

2 Bring the working end alongside the standing part of the line and then double it back on itself to make a bight.

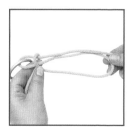

3 Take the working end up and around the two standing parts in a wrapping turn.

4 Make three more wrapping turns and then bring the working end of the line up and through the bight.

5 Tighten the knot by pulling on the working end.

6 Draw the knot to the eye by holding the hook securely and pulling on the standing part of the line.

Universal loop

Even stronger than the double version because of the extra turn, this loop is most often used for tying snoods — short lengths of monofilament that carry hooks and are attached to the trace or booms.

TYPE OF KNOT

HITCH

USE

ATTACHING SNOODS

OTHER NAMES

TRIPLE OVERHAND LOOP

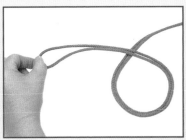

1 Make a long bight in the end of a length of cord. Form a loop in the doubled end.

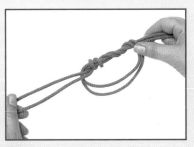

2 Now tie a triple overhand knot (see page 22).

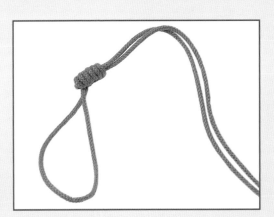

3 Using your fingers, finally work out any unevenness in the knot to make a smooth, barrel-shaped knot.

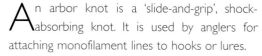

TYPE OF KNOT

HITCH

USE

JOINING LINES TO TACKLE

OTHER NAMES

NONE

An arbor knot is a 'slide-and-grip', shock-absorbing knot. It is used by anglers for attaching monofilament lines to hooks or lures.

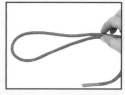

1 In one end of a line, make a bight.

2 With the working end lying across the parallel parts of the line, form a small loop.

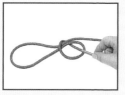

3 Now take the working end behind and through the loop.

4 Bring the working end over the two parallel parts of the line and make a complete round turn around them.

5 Make another complete round turn by taking the working end behind once again. Ensure that you keep the wrappings tight as you turn. Making sure that all of the turns lie closely together, make a third round turn with the working end.

6 Tighten the small loop and pull on one of the large loop legs to trap the end.

Policansky knot

This knot is much favoured by sea fishermen, particularly those with enough patience and muscle to tackle giant fish like the skate. The Policansky knot is used to attach Dacron line to big-game swivels. It's a little fiddly to do at first, but does get easier with practice.

TYPE OF KNOT

HITCH

USE

JOINING LINES TO TACKLE

OTHER NAMES

NONE

1 Pass the working end of the line through the eye of the swivel from back to front. Keep the working end quite long.

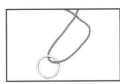

2 Bring the working end around the back of the standing part.

3 Take the working end over the standing part so that it lies on top of the leg of the loop.

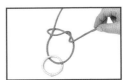

4 Take the working end around the leg of the loop in a wrapping turn.

5 Continue to wrap the working end over the leg of the loop in wrapping turns. Keep the turns neat and close to each other, but not too tight.

6 Continue to make wrapping turns all the way around the loop. The size of the loop may need to be adjusted. Do this by very gently pulling on the standing part of the line: notice how the wrapping turns are drawn closely together.

7 Finish the knot with a half-hitch and trim off the tag end.

SECTION

4

SAILING KNOTS

ROPE DOES NOT PLAY THE SAME VITAL PART ABOARD SHIPS
TODAY AS ONCE IT DID. KNOT-TYING ON BOARD THE VESSELS
OF THE 18TH AND 19TH CENTURIES WAS OFTEN VERY COM-
PETITIVE, AND SAILORS JEALOUSLY GUARDED THE 'SECRETS'
OF PARTICULAR KNOTS. SAILORS WERE RESPONSIBLE FOR A
GREAT PROPORTION OF THE MANY KNOTS IN EXISTENCE, AND
FOR THEIR DESCRIPTIVE AND COLOURFUL NAMES. TODAY, IT
IS STILL VITAL THAT ANY SAILOR — WHETHER OF A SMALL
DINGHY OR A SLEEK, RACING YACHT — IS ABLE TO MAKE THE
CORRECT KNOT FOR THE APPROPRIATE PURPOSE. THE SAFETY
OF THE VESSEL, CREW AND PASSENGERS MAY WELL DEPEND
ON THE ABILITY TO MAKE A KNOT. THE KNOTS DEMONSTRAT-
ED HERE ARE SOME OF THE MOST USEFUL AND WILL HELP TO
TURN THE MOST HOPELESS OF LANDLUBBERS INTO EFFICIENT
DECKHANDS. IT IS IMPORTANT TO FOLLOW THE STEP-BY-STEP
METHOD, AS REVERSING OR CHANGING THE ORDER MAY
RESULT IN A COMPLETELY DIFFERENT KNOT, ONE THAT MAY
BE INSECURE AND CONSEQUENTLY UNSAFE. WITH ALL KNOT-
TYING, PATIENCE AND PRACTICE ARE VITAL: UNDERSTAND THE
FUNCTION AND APPLICATIONS OF EACH KNOT AND PRACTICE
IT UNTIL YOU ARE CONFIDENT THAT YOU CAN TIE IT IN A
STORM! IF YOU ARE IN DOUBT, ALWAYS ASK AN EXPERIENCED
SHIPMATE FOR ASSISTANCE.

4 Reef knot

TYPE OF KNOT

BEND

USE

JOINING TWO LINES

OTHER NAMES

SQUARE KNOT, TRUE KNOT,
HARD KNOT, FLAT KNOT,
ORDINARY KNOT

Remember the sequence:
'left over right and under;
right over left and under', and
you'll have a reef knot every
time. This granny knot is not
what you are aiming for!

This is one of the oldest knots and one that most people know how to tie. The reef knot gets its name from its nautical use of tying two ends of a rope when reefing (tying up) a sail. The reef knot is not a secure bend and should never be used as one. Nor should it be tied with ropes of different diameter. The reef knot is properly tied using the two ends of the same rope to make a temporary join. Often mistaken for the insecure and best-avoided granny knot, a correctly tied reef knot is symmetrical, with both short ends finishing on the same side.

1 Take the two ends of the same line.

2 Take the left-hand end over the right-hand end, under and back over in a half-knot.

3 Place the right-hand end over, under and back over the left-hand end so that you tie a second half-knot.

4 Tighten the knot by pulling on the two ends of the rope.

Sheet bend

The sheet bend is among the most widely used bends. It is unusual in that it can be tied using two different-diameter ropes. It is not, however, a secure knot, especially in synthetic rope, and can work loose if the rope is jerked about too much. It should never be used in circumstances where great strain is put on the ropes. Remember, too, that the breaking strength will also decrease in direct proportion to the difference of the lines joined.

TYPE OF KNOT

BEND

USE

JOINING TWO LINES

OTHER NAMES

COMMON BEND, FLAG BEND

1 In the end of one of the ropes, make a large bight.

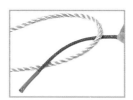

2 Tuck the end of the second rope up through the bight in the first rope.

3 Pass the working end of the second rope under this bight.

4 Making sure that both short ends are situated on the same side of the completed knot, tuck the working end under its own standing part.

5 Pull on the standing part of the second rope to tighten the knot. Trim the working ends to length if desired.

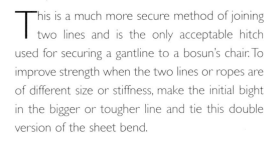

TYPE OF KNOT

BEND

USE

JOINING TWO LINES

OTHER NAMES

NONE

This is a much more secure method of joining two lines and is the only acceptable hitch used for securing a gantline to a bosun's chair. To improve strength when the two lines or ropes are of different size or stiffness, make the initial bight in the bigger or tougher line and tie this double version of the sheet bend.

1 Make a bight in the end of the larger of the ropes to be tied.

2 Take the second rope and tuck its end up through the bight in the first rope.

3 Pass the working end of the second rope under the bight.

4 Tuck the working end under itself, making sure that both short ends are situated on the same side of the knot.

5 Bring the working end around and beneath the bight and its own standing part once again, making sure that you keep it to the right of the original pass.

6 Tuck the end through and alongside the initial tuck to complete the double knot.

7 Tighten the knot by pulling on the standing part of the second rope. Trim the working ends if desired.

Heaving-line bend

First mentioned in 1912 in a Swedish knot manual, *De Viktigaste Knutarna*, by Hjalmar Ohrvall, this quick and easy knot is used to attach a lightweight throwing or messenger line to the bight or eye of a heavier hawser (heavy rope) that is to be hauled into position.

TYPE OF KNOT

BEND

USE

JOINING TWO LINES

OTHER NAMES

NONE

1 Make a bight in the larger rope.

2 Lay the lighter line over this bight so that the working ends of both ropes are next to each other.

3 Bring the working end of the lighter line around and under the standing part of the bight. Then bring it over its own standing part.

4 Now take the working end of the lighter line under the short leg of the bight.

5 Take the working end of the lighter line back over the two legs of the bight and tuck it underneath itself.

TYPE OF KNOT

BEND

USE

JOINING TWO LINES

OTHER NAMES

HUNTER'S BEND

The rigger's bend, or hunter's bend, is based on two overhand knots. It's a useful, general-purpose sailing knot, with a good grip. Stronger than either the reef knot or the sheet bend, it's also simple to untie.

1 Position the two lines parallel and next to one another. The working ends must face in opposite directions.

2 Make a twin loop, keeping the two rope parts parallel at all times.

3 Bring the working end currently at the front of the loops around to the back. Tuck this working end through the loop, from back to front.

4 Take the other working end to the front of the two loops.

5 Now tuck this working end through the loop, from the front to the back.

6 Start to remove any slack from the knot, ensuring that the working ends do not come out of the loops.

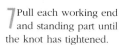

7 Pull each working end and standing part until the knot has tightened.

Cleating a line

Acleat is a deck fitting to which lines are tied temporarily, being made fast by a hitch. A very simple, yet effective, hitch, it's also one that many landlubbers tie incorrectly. Most people wrongly believe that the more turns put around the cleat, the stronger the hitch. In fact, when tied properly, this hitch only needs a couple of turns to be both secure and quickly untied.

TYPE OF KNOT

HITCH

USE

MOORING/FASTENING

OTHER NAMES

NONE

1 Take the working end of the line around the top end of the cleat and down the side in a clockwise direction (or, as sailors say, 'with the sun') and then under the bottom end of the cleat.

2 Take the working end over and across the 'spine' of the cleat (anti-clockwise, or against the sun) and under the top end, making the top part of a figure-of-eight. Take the working end up and over so that it lies across the spine of the cleat, trapping the part of the rope underneath.

3 Take the working end under the lower end of the cleat and then up and across, tucking it under the rope to finish the figure-of-eight.

TYPE OF KNOT

HITCH

USE

MOORING/FASTENING

OTHER NAMES

BOATMAN'S KNOT, PEG KNOT

One of the best-known and most useful hitches aboard a yacht, the clove hitch can be used to fasten a line to a rail, spar or another rope. With practice, it should be possible to tie this knot with just one hand. The clove hitch is not, however, a totally secure mooring knot: it will work loose if put under intermittent strain, especially from different angles. Make it more secure by adding a stopper knot or a couple of half-hitches around the standing part of the rope.

1 Take the working end of a line around the anchor point, from front to back.

2 Take this working end up and diagonally across the front of the standing part.

3 To trap the standing part, bring the working end down, behind the back of the anchor point.

4 Tuck the working end up beneath the diagonal crossing.

5 To tighten the knot, pull on the standing part of the rope.

Pile hitch

A practical and neat way to moor a boat temporarily, the pile hitch is also remarkably secure. It's ideal for attaching ropes to a post because the loop can be passed over the top.

TYPE OF KNOT

HITCH

USE

MOORING/FASTENING

OTHER NAMES

NONE

1 First make a bight in the rope.

2 Take this bight over the post.

3 Take the bight around the front of the post and under both standing parts of the rope.

4 Loop the bight over the post. If required, the two legs of the line can now be led off in different directions.

4 | Buntline hitch

TYPE OF KNOT

HITCH

USE

MOORING/FASTENING

OTHER NAMES

NONE

This hitch is specifically used for attaching buntlines to the eyes or eyelet holes in sails. In order that it does not work loose in strong winds, the buntline hitch needs to be secure. Its strength comes from the short working end being trapped inside the knot.

1 Take the working end of the line through the eyehole, from back to front, and pull some line through.

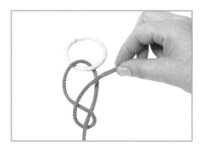

2 Take the working end across the front of the standing part, then around the back and across over the front in a figure-of-eight pattern.

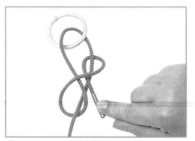

3 Take the working end up and behind the standing part and pass it through the small loop formed.

4 Tuck the working end under its own standing part and tighten the knot by pulling on the working end and standing part.

Constrictor knot

This is another popular general-purpose knot because of its firmness and its grip. Its nautical use is usually to make temporary whipping on the ends of rope to stop them from fraying. It can be tied in the end or on a bight and is a difficult knot to untie.

TYPE OF KNOT

HITCH

USE

WHIPPING/MOORING

OTHER NAMES

NONE

1 Arrange a length of rope around the object to be tied.

2 Take the working end of the rope up, over its own standing part.

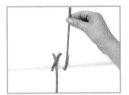

3 Bring the working end down at the back and then up at the front.

4 Complete a clove hitch by tucking the working end under the diagonal made earlier.

5 Find the upper left-hand knot part and slightly loosen it. Tuck the working end through the loosened bight, from left to right.

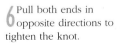

6 Pull both ends in opposite directions to tighten the knot.

7 Cut off the knot er close to the kno'

Because sailors 'bent' ropes to anchors, the knots they used were misleadingly called bends. The fisherman's bend is, in fact, a hitch. It is related to the round turn and two half-hitches, but is a much more secure hitch, particularly when the rope is wet or slippery. A more permanent hitch can be achieved by seizing the working end to the standing part of the rope.

1 Pass a long working end twice through the ring to form a complete round turn.

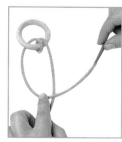

2 Take the working end down and across the standing part.

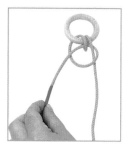

3 Form a locking half-hitch around the standing part by tucking the working end through the round turn.

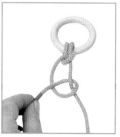

4 Tie a second, identical half-hitch.

5 Pull on the working end and standing part to tighten the knot.

Rolling hitch

This is a useful knot for mariners as it is the most effective way of securing a small rope to a larger line that is under strain. As long as the smaller rope is perpendicular to the larger rope, the knot will slide. But once tension is exerted on the standing part and working end of the smaller rope, the knot locks into position. For windsurfers, this knot is essential: it is this that secures the wishbone boom to the mast.

TYPE OF KNOT

HITCH

USE

MOORING/FASTENING

OTHER NAMES

MAGNER'S HITCH,
MAGNUS HITCH

1 Pass the working end of the smaller line, from front to back, around the anchorage.

2 Take the working end up and diagonally across the front of the standing part.

3 Bring the working end down behind the anchorage once more and then out so that it emerges between the diagonal and the standing part.

4 Make a second diagonal turn beside the first one and bring the working end behind the anchorage again.

5 Tuck the working end up through the second diagonal turn. Pull on the working end and the standing part.

TYPE OF KNOT

HITCH

USE

LIFTING HEAVY LOADS

OTHER NAMES

NONE

Because the strain is equal on both sides, the cat's paw lessens the chance of the rope weakening. Should one leg accidentally break, the other can take the weight of the load, allowing it to be lowered safely. It's the best hook knot for rope of medium diameter.

1 Double a length of rope to make a bight.

2 Make a pair of matching loops by bringing the end of the bight down, over the standing parts.

3 Twist the left-hand loop clockwise, then twist the right-hand loop anti-clockwise.

4 Add two or three more twists to each of the loops.

5 Insert the anchorage through both of these twisted loops.

6 To straighten the standing parts of the rope, pull on them. Then slide the wrapping turns up to lie snugly against the anchorage.

Marlinespike hitch

Marlines are salt-water 'big-game' fish, with a long, pointed, spear-like structure on their upper jaws. A marlinespike is the same shape! In this hitch, the marlinespike is useful for pulling thin line without it biting into your hands. Once the knot is no longer needed, the marlinespike is simply removed and the knot disappears.

TYPE OF KNOT

HITCH

USE

PULLING THIN LINES

OTHER NAMES

NONE

1 Lay the spike on top of a length of rope, fixed at one end.

2 Lift the rope upwards to lie over the tool.

3 Twist the tool upwards, clockwise. Insert the point behind the standing part.

4 Lift the crossing turn that has formed around the tool up, towards the standing part of the rope.

5 Pull the standing part through the crossing turn with the point of the tool. Push the tool further through the knot and, with one or both hands, apply strain to the rope by pulling down on the tool, thus avoiding injuring your hands.

4 Bowline

TYPE OF KNOT

LOOP

USE

RESCUE/MAKING EYES

OTHER NAMES

NONE

The bowline (pronounced 'boh-lin') is one of the best-known and most widely used knots to make a fixed loop at the end of a line or to attach a rope to an object. Simple to tie, yet very strong and stable, it is also easy to untie by pushing forward the bight that goes around the standing part of the line.

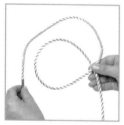

1 Bring a long working end across the rope's standing part to form an overhand loop.

2 Bring the working end from front to back through the crossing turn and leave a long loop in the working end.

3 Bring the working end behind the standing part of the rope.

4 Next pass the working end from front to back up through the crossing turn.

5 Pull on the standing part and the doubled working end to tighten the knot.

Bowline on a bight

This bowline tied on the bight produces two fixed loops which overlap each other. When they are pulled apart, each can be used separately. Used especially in rescues at sea, a conscious victim passes a leg through each loop and hangs on tight to the standing part. An unconscious victim has both legs passed through a single loop, while the other loop goes under the armpits.

TYPE OF KNOT

LOOP

USE

RESCUE

OTHER NAMES

NONE

1 Form a bight by doubling a long length of rope.

2 Take the bight over the standing parts to make a crossing turn.

3 Pass the bight from back to front through the crossing turn.

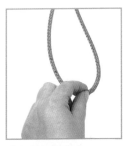

4 Open out the bight and pull it down to extend just below the loop. Leave a double-stranded loop.

5 Take the bight over, then behind, the loop and crossing turn. Next take it up behind the standing parts.

6 Pull on the standing parts and on the strands of the loop below the crossing turn to tighten the knot.

TYPE OF KNOT

LOOP

USE

RESCUE/MAKING EYES

OTHER NAMES

NONE

On old sailing ships, the running bowline was used to tighten the square sail to the yard-arm. Today, this is probably the only running knot used by sailors: as well as on running rigging, it is used to retrieve floating objects that have fallen overboard. The weight of the object creates the tension that makes the knot tight.

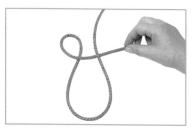

1 Make two bights in the working end of the line, as shown.

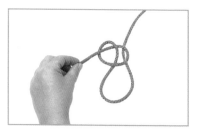

2 Bring the working end over the first standing part and then under the second standing part of the line.

3 Take the working end over the standing part and through the upper loop from back to front, so that it lies outside and alongside the lower loop. Take the working end around the leg of the lower loop from back to front and up through the small eye so that it lies alongside its own standing part.

4 Tighten the knot by pulling gently on the working end of the rope and on the lower loop.

Figure-of-eight knot

This knot gets its name from its characteristic shape. At sea, it is used as a stopper knot on running rigging — the ropes that are used to lift sails and yards. It has long been used as a symbol of 'interwoven' affection. In heraldry, it was used as the symbol of faithful love and also appears on the arms of the House of Savoy, giving rise to one of its alternative names.

TYPE OF KNOT

STOPPER

USE

BINDING ENDS, WEIGHTING LINES, PREVENTING SLIPPAGE

OTHER NAMES

FLEMISH KNOT, SAVOY KNOT

1 At the end of a rope, make a small bight.

2 Turn the bight into a loop by giving it a half-twist.

3 Make the figure-of-eight-shaped elbow by making a second half-twist.

4 Pass the working end through the loop.

5 Pull on both ends of the line to tighten the knot.

SECTION

5

HOUSEHOLD KNOTS

WE HAVE BECOME USED TO THE BENEFITS OF ADHESIVE
TAPE FOR WRAPPING UP PACKAGES AND STAPLE AND NAIL
GUNS FOR FAST REPAIRS, WHILE VELCRO FASTENINGS
MEAN THAT WE DON'T EVEN HAVE TO TIE OUR
SHOELACES! NEVERTHELESS, IN EVEN THE MOST HIGH-
TECH HOME, WORKSHOP, GARAGE OR POTTING SHED,
YOU'LL FIND A BALL OF STRING! WHERE WOULD WE BE
WITHOUT A ROPE FOR A WASHING LINE OR STRING FOR
FLYING A KITE? WHERE WOULD GARDENERS BE WITHOUT
SOFT TWINE FOR TYING CLIMBING PLANTS TO THEIR
SUPPORTS? WHAT WOULD A ROAST DINNER BE LIKE IF
'CHEF' COULDN'T ROLL AND TIE A JOINT OF MEAT?
LIKE THE TASKS OF THE MARINER, ANGLER AND
MOUNTAINEER, MANY JOBS AROUND THE GARDEN AND
HOME CAN ONLY BE UNDERTAKEN WITH ROPE, CORD OR
'SMALL STUFF' LIKE STRING. AND WITH A JUDICIOUS
CHOICE OF MATERIALS, MANY MUNDANE TASKS CAN BE
MADE BOTH MORE PLEASURABLE AND MORE BEAUTIFUL.
REMEMBER, TOO, THAT WHEN YOU REMOVE THAT PIECE
OF ADHESIVE TAPE, ITS 'STICK' IS GONE AND IT CAN'T BE
USED AGAIN. UNTIE A KNOT, ON THE OTHER HAND, AND
IN MOST CASES THE ROPE, CORD OR STRING CAN BE
USED AGAIN TIME AND TIME AGAIN.

5 Granny knot

TYPE OF KNOT

LOOP

USE

TYING SHOELACES

OTHER NAMES

FALSE KNOT,

BOOBY KNOT,

LUBBER'S KNOT

Although it is somewhat unreliable — it either slips or jams because both half-knots are tied in the same direction — the granny knot has to be the most widely used knot. With added twin drawloops, it's probably the first knot we all learn to tie to fasten our shoelaces. The granny-knot sequence is easy to remember: left over right and under, left over right and under. Kids will soon learn to tie their laces if you nail a spare set to a wall so that they can practice tying them.

1 Taking the two ends of a piece of webbing or cord, cross the left-hand end over the right-hand one.

2 Pass the left-hand end under and back up over the right-hand end to tie a half-knot.

3 Bringing the ends together again, cross the left-hand end over the right-hand end.

4 Pass the left-hand end under and back up over the right-hand end to tie a second half-knot.

5 Pull on both ends to tighten the knot.

Plank sling

When you've run out of wall and floor space for storage, all that's left is the ceiling. But make sure that any ceiling hooks are attached securely before suspending objects from them. The plank sling was originally used by carpenters for staging, using strong rope for added strength. A single knot in the middle of a plank is useful for hauling it up a short distance. Knots at either end will allow you to suspend the plank horizontally.

TYPE OF KNOT

HITCH

USE

SUSPENDING OBJECTS

OTHER NAMES

NONE

1 Lay a plank over one end of the rope.

2 Make an 'S' shape by pushing and then push an extra bight under the plank.

3 Take one end of the rope over the plank. Tuck it through the bight on the opposite side of the plank.

4 Bring the other end of rope over the plank and tuck it through its opposite bight.

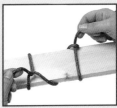

5 Tighten and adjust the sling so that the bight tips are just above the edge of the plank.

6 Secure the standing part of the rope to the shorter end of the rope.

TYPE OF KNOT

BEND

USE

BINDING OBJECTS

OTHER NAMES

NONE

If the object to be bound has a large diameter — a big parcel, for example — or if there are several objects to be bound together that don't 'naturally' pull together, the double version of the constrictor knot is most useful because it has additional internal friction and extra grip.

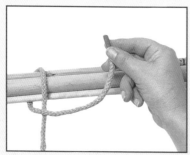

1 Wrap the cord around the item(s) to be secured. Bring the working end up diagonally and take it across its own standing part.

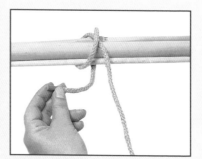

2 Lead the working end down, behind the foundation object(s), and then up in front once more, taking care to keep between the standing part of the rope and the first turn.

3 Take the working end up and around the foundation again, doubling the diagonal overlay.

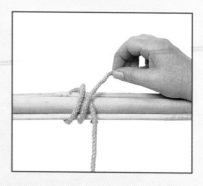

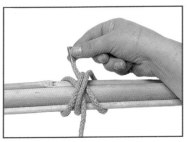

4 Pass the working end directly down, behind the foundation, to emerge on the right-hand side of the standing part. Tuck the working end through the two turns so that it lies parallel to, and to the right of, its own standing part.

5 Find and loosen the upper left-hand part of the knot.

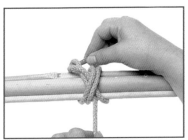

6 Bring the working end across and tuck it from left to right through the loosened bight.

7 Pull on both ends as tightly as possible and cut off the ends close to the knot.

5 Boa knot

Not only practical, the boa knot is more decorative than a constrictor knot.

I Make an overhand loop in a short length of cord or rope.

2 Add a second turn so that it rests on top of the first turn.

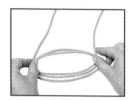

3 Arrange these loops into a coil, with both ends lying in the same direction. You should have three cord parts under each thumb.

4 Lift and rotate the three right-hand cord parts through 180° to create a figure-of-eight shape. Check that each loop, and the top overlying diagonal, has three strands around it, with just two strands beneath it.

5 Insert the end of the object beneath one of the end loops.

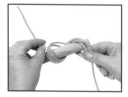

6 Slide the object over the centre crossing and push it carefully through the other loop.

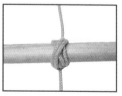

7 Work the knot into shape, pulling on the ends to tighten it.

This knot is useful when you have to tie a rope to an 'anchor' with a large diameter, such as a tree branch. Any movement or vibration on the standing part of the rope tightens the knot.

TYPE OF KNOT

HITCH

USE

BINDING, TOWING

OTHER NAMES

NONE

1 Pass the working end of the line from front to back around the anchor point.

2 Bring the working end underneath its own standing part, diagonally up and to the right.

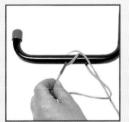

3 Bring the working end up, over and down the back of the object.

4 Bring the working end across the front of its standing part, then, from left to right, up through the underlying diagonal.

5 Bring the working end over the overlying knot part and tuck it underneath the diagonal crossing again.

6 Tug on the standing part to tighten the knot. Any further vibrations will tighten it.

TYPE OF KNOT

HITCH

USE

SUSPENDING ITEMS,

HAULING, TOWING

OTHER NAMES

NONE

The first part of this knot combination, the timber hitch, is still used by woodsmen and lumberjacks to haul felled trees.

1 Pass a long working end of rope up around the back of the object and then down over the front.

2 Bring the working end around its own standing part and form a small loop.

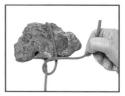

3 Tuck the working end through itself and the standing part.

4 Take the working end around its own standing part again.

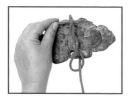

5 Make a second tuck with the working end between the standing part and itself.

6 Tighten the newly formed noose by pulling on the standing part. This is the basic timber hitch.

7 To convert it into a killick hitch, make a half-hitch near the end of the object. This acts as a stabiliser and stops the load from swaying.

Sheepshank

If you can't cut a rope, a sheepshank is the best temporary way to shorten it. This knot is also useful for taking the strain off a damaged, worn or 'suspect' piece of rope: tie a sheepshank with the weakened section of rope in the middle of the knot so that the strain can be taken on the other two standing parts.

TYPE OF KNOT

HITCH

USE

SHORTENING ROPE

OTHER NAMES

NONE

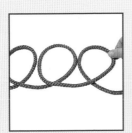

1 Make three crossing turns along the line, all in the same direction.

2 Pull the right-hand leg of the central crossing turn through the back of the right-hand crossing turn and pull the left-hand leg through the front of the left-hand crossing turn.

3 Pull on the newly formed loops and then on the standing parts of the rope.

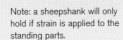

Note: a sheepshank will only hold if strain is applied to the standing parts.

TYPE OF KNOT

BINDING

USE

LASHING

OTHER NAMES

NONE

Here's a simple way to secure any number of long objects together — curtain poles, spare broom handles and garden canes can all be kept tidy in storage. It's useful for binding tent poles together at the end of a camping trip, too. Repeat these steps with a second length of cord at the other end of the object.

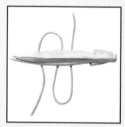

1 Arrange the cord underneath, and close to the end of, the objects to be tied, in an 'S' shape.

2 Bring one end of the cord over the objects and then down through the opposite bight.

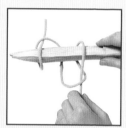

3 Bring the other end of the cord over the objects and down through the other bight.

4 To draw the cord and the objects tightly together, pull both ends.

5 Now cross the left end over the right end and pull tight.

6 Bring the ends back together and cross the right over the left.

Double figure-of-eight hitch

An alternative to both the boa and constrictor knots, this is an easy-to-remember figure-of-eight binding knot.

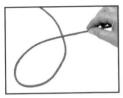

1 With one end of a length of cord, first make a clockwise overhand loop.

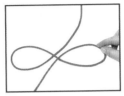

2 Now form a figure-of-eight shape by adding an anti-clockwise overhand loop.

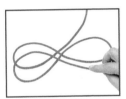

3 Now lay a second clockwise overhand loop on top of the first.

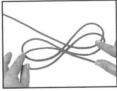

4 Taking the other end of the cord, lay a second clockwise overhand loop on top of the first.

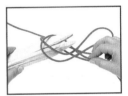

5 Slide the object through the left-hand loops and over the crossing turns.

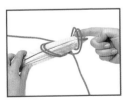

6 Now pass the object through the right-hand pair of loops.

7 Position the knot where you require it on the object and pull on both ends to tighten it.

Although it looks complex, this rope ladder is actually quite easy to tie and would make a great finishing touch to a tree house. The rungs are simply running knots secured at both sides, so it is important to make sure that the turns are well tightened. You may want to use pins and polystyrene to secure it in place as you work.

1 Double a long length of sturdy rope and then, in the bight, tie a figure-of-eight knot (see page 95).

2 Separate the two ends of the rope and lay them parallel to determine the width of the rungs.

3 Take the left-hand rope over to the right-hand rope, pass it under and around it and then back over to the left side again.

4 Make a second bight in the left-hand rope and lay it alongside the first, then pass the working left end behind the right-hand rope.

5 Take the right-hand rope up behind both bights and make a series of wrapping turns, trapping all of the parts of the bights. Make sure that all of the turns are well tightened and lie snugly against each other.

6 At the end of the rung, pass the working end of the right-hand rope down through the loop remaining in the wrapped bight. You've now made the first rung of your rope ladder.

7 Make the next rung in the same manner, but this time start the process with the right-hand rope.

8 Make as many rungs as you need, each time alternating between left- and right-hand ropes.

6

CRAFT KNOTS

THERE ARE JUST A FEW OF THE ENORMOUS
NUMBER OF DECORATIVE KNOTS IN THIS SECTION,
AMONG THEM PLAITS, SENNITS AND STOPPER KNOTS. A
PLAIT IS MADE UP OF A NUMBER OF STRANDS OF ROPE
THAT ARE INTERWOVEN IN A SIMPLE, REPEATING
PATTERN, WHILE A SENNIT IS CREATED BY A MORE
COMPLEX PATTERN. BOTH CREATE DECORATIVE KNOTS, AS
WELL AS STRONG LENGTHS OF ROPE. STOPPER KNOTS
ARE ALSO KNOWN AS 'KNOB KNOTS' AND ARE GENERALLY
TIED AS A TERMINAL KNOT IN THE END OF A ROPE TO
STOP IT FROM SLIPPING THROUGH AN EYE OR A HOLE.
AMONG THE MORE COMPLEX PATTERNS ARE MATS TO
MAKE, AS WELL AS A HAMMOCK TO GRACE YOUR
GARDEN. AS WITH ALL KNOTS, PRACTICE MAKES PERFECT!
AND REMEMBER, IT'S A LOT EASIER TO PRACTISE USING
SOME STOUT, QUITE THICK, ROPE.

TYPE OF KNOT

BEND

USE

DECORATIVE

OTHER NAMES

RUSTLER'S KNOT

CHINESE GOOD-LUCK KNOT

JAPANESE CROWN KNOT

This knot looks terrific tied in two contrasting-coloured ropes or used as curtain tie-backs. Try tying a neck scarf in this way, too!

1 In the end of one cord, make a bight. Pass this bight over the end of the other cord.

2 Bring the working end of the second cord up behind the bight in the first cord.

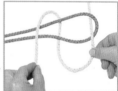

3 Take the working end of the second cord down over, and in front of, the bight made in the first cord.

4 Bring the working end of the first cord over the front of the second cord, making a locking tuck through the bight.

5 Gently pull on each of the four strands in turn to flatten and tighten the knot.

6 Add some more square knots on top of the first knot and admire the effect!

Turk's head (FLAT FORM)

Turk's heads are very attractive knots — even Leonardo da Vinci was fascinated by them and drew a number in his notebooks in the 15th century. They are most commonly tied around a cylindrical object like a boat tiller — in most cases as pure decoration. This version is the flat form, which creates an attractive mat. You could, however, turn it down and work it over a cylinder to form a decorative covering.

TYPE OF KNOT

LOOP

USE

DECORATIVE

OTHER NAMES

NONE

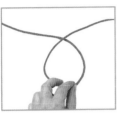

1 Middle a length of cord and make an anti-clockwise overhand loop in the working end.

2 Bring the working end down, behind the loop, and arrange it in a 'pretzel' layout.

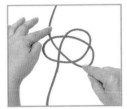

3 Pick up the other end of the cord and thread it diagonally up and to the left, going over, under, then over, the knot parts.

4 Lead the end around clockwise and thread it diagonally to the right, going under, over, under and over.

5 Take the end alongside the standing part and follow the original lead around again to double the knot. (You could make a third turn if you like.) Fix the end in place either with glue or a stitch on the underside of the mat.

TYPE OF KNOT

LOOP

USE

DECORATIVE

OTHER NAMES

NONE

This knot is very eye-catching, but also easy to tie. A useful way to make the bights even is to use a flat piece of polystyrene and some pins to hold the rope in place as you arrange it. It's also easier to make using stiff cord.

1 Middle a length of cord and make a narrow bight.

2 Pull out a second bight in the left-hand leg of the cord, keeping one finger at the bottom of the original bight. Make this bight the same size as the first.

3 In the right-hand leg of the cord, make a third bight the same size as the other two bights.

4 Now lay both of the cord's standing parts over the left-hand bight.

5 Take the end of the left-hand bight and lay it over the upper bight.

6 Take the end of the upper bight and lay it over both of the bights lying on the right-hand side of the knot.

Good-luck knot

7 Take the lower, right-hand bight and bring it over the downward-pointing bight. Tuck this bight through, beneath the two standing parts of the cord.

8 Without distorting its shape, carefully tighten the four-part crown.

9 Now bring the left-hand bight down over the lower bight diagonally and then bring the lower bight over it.

10 Take the right-hand bight over what is now the upper bight.

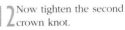
12 Now tighten the second crown knot.

11 Lead the two strands of the standing parts over the left-hand bight. Tuck this under the two strands of the 'bent-over' lower bight.

Craft knots • **115**

TYPE OF KNOT

LOOP

USE

DECORATIVE

OTHER NAMES

NONE

This decorative flat mat is quick and easy to tie. These make ideal mats for placing hot pans on in the kitchen or can be used as part of other furnishing projects.

1 First make an overhand loop in a length of cord.

2 Make a pretzel shape by bringing the working end down over the loop.

3 Take the working end behind the standing part, moving it from right to left.

4 Thread the working end clockwise around, and through, the knot, going over-under-over-under the rope parts.

5 Tuck the working end alongside, and parallel to, the standing part. Now follow the original lead around once (or twice) again to double (or triple) the knot.

Four-strand braid

This method of braiding produces a flat, open, ornamental 'network' of rope that can be used as a decorative border on curtains or upholstery. Alternatively, its flatness makes it ideal for making belts or even replacement straps for shoulder and shopping bags.

TYPE OF KNOT

BRAID

USE

LASHING

OTHER NAMES

NONE

1 Middle two lengths of rope. Pass one loop through the other. Separate the four strands into a right-hand and a left-hand pair.

2 First work with the left-hand pair. Cross the left-hand strand over the right-hand strand, left over right.

3 Now move to the right-hand pair. Cross the left-hand strand over the right-hand strand, also left over right.

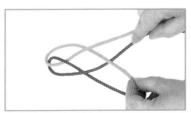

4 Now cross the innermost strands right over left.

5 Repeat steps 2, 3 and 4. Remember to maintain tension and tightness in the cords, otherwise the pattern will not be symmetrical. Continue crossing over the strands to the required length. Bind the ends together.

LOOP

DECORATIVE

NONE

This a classic flat, decorative knot. Again, securing the rope with pins to polystyrene can be helpful. The pattern is made more solid by following the lead around. However, the actual size of the knot can only be increased by adding more bights — six or nine bights would make a long ocean plait! Remember that you will need quite a long length of rope.

1 Make an anti-clockwise overhand loop in one end of a fairly long length of line.

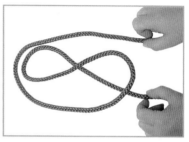

2 Bending the long working end around to the left, lay it over the standing end of the original loop.

3 Now bring the end up and lay it from left to right over the top loop. Take the working end diagonally down, from right to left, laying it on top of the lower loop.

4 Taking the other half of the line (this is now your new working end), lay it from left to right over the new standing part of rope.

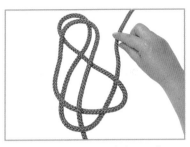

5 Bring the working end diagonally up and to the right, going under, then under again, the nearest loop.

6 Bring the working end diagonally from right to left, over, then under, then over and under again, all of the knot parts.

7 Bring the working end diagonally from left to right, over, under, over, under and over the knot parts to emerge at the bottom right of the mat.

8 Tuck the working end up alongside, and parallel to, the standing part. Follow the lead around once (or twice) more to double (or triple) the knot.

TYPE OF KNOT

SENNIT

USE

DECORATIVE

OTHER NAMES

NONE

This sennit is made by tying a series of crown knots — all tied in the same direction.

1 Bind four ropes together at one end.

2 Working in an anti-clockwise direction, pick up one strand and pass it over the second, leaving a small bight.

3 Working in the same direction, pick up the second strand and pass it over the first and third strands.

4 Pass the third strand over the second and fourth strands.

5 Pick up the fourth strand, pass it over the third strand and through the bight formed between the first and second strands. This forms a four-strand crown knot. Tighten by pulling each rope.

6 Repeat steps 2 to 5, always working in an anti-clockwise direction and tightening each knot as it is made. Continue making additional crown knots until the desired length is achieved and then bind the ends.

Heaving-line knot

A heaving-line knot is one of the most decorative knots and its alternative names are derived from the fact that these knots weight the cords worn by Franciscan monks as belts. In sailing, it is used when a heavy line has to be thrown ashore or aboard another boat. This heavy rope is attached first to a heaving line — a light line which is thrown ahead so that the heavier line can be hauled across the gap.

TYPE OF KNOT

HITCH

USE

DECORATIVE/SAILING

OTHER NAMES

MONK'S KNOT,

FRANCISCAN'S KNOT

1 Leaving a long working end, make a fairly large bight.

2 Take the working end over the standing part and up and around the back of the bight.

3 Take the working end over the bight to make a round turn.

4 Make three more turns around the bight with the working end.

5 Tuck the working end through the bight and pull it through.

6 Pull the knot tight and work it into shape so that the turns lie snugly and neatly side by side in the finished knot.

STOPPER KNOT

USE

DECORATIVE,

HEAVING-LINE KNOT

OTHER NAMES

NONE

This is one of the most decorative knots, but it also has a practical purpose as it is generally tied at the end of a heaving line. It also makes a very attractive knob knot at the end of any cord. It is easier to make in larger, stiffer stuff, so practise it first using some spare rope. In small stuff, it makes a terrific key fob.

1 Make three turns around one hand, working towards the end of the rope.

2 Slip the turns off your hand and turn the rope at right angles across the complete turns and make a second cycle of three turns across the first. Hold the rope in place with your thumb.

3 Tuck the rope through the first cycle of turns, next to the second. Pull the rope to tighten the final third turn of the second cycle.

4 Take the rope over the second cycle of turns and tuck it back through the first cycle, pulling the rope slowly through.

5 Make three turns around the second cycle, tucking them through the first cycle of turns (as in steps 3 and 4). Lay the three turns over the rope where it changes direction to anchor the underlying rope parts in place.

4 If you wish, you could either insert a small ball into the centre of the knot or tuck the working end down into the core, out of sight. Carefully and patiently work the monkey's fist into its distinctive spherical shape.

Hammock

Hammocks are made of a mesh of net tied to a frame rope called a 'headline'. This rope has to be strong enough to take all of the strain from the net, so select a strong, thick rope. The mesh can be tied to the headline using clove hitches (see page 84) and sheet bends (page 79).

TYPE OF KNOT

CLOVE HITCH/SHEET BEND

USE

SUSPENSION/RELAXATION

OTHER NAMES

NONE

1 Lay out the rope for the headline in the shape and proportions required Working from the top left-hand corner of the headline, tie in mesh rope with a clove hitch. Make a small bight and then tie a second clove hitch.

2 At the right-hand corner, secure the mesh rope to the top edge with a clove hitch, then bring the mesh twine down the right-hand edge and tie another clove hitch.

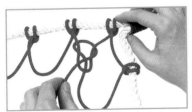

3 Working from right to left, take the mesh rope across to the bight and tie a sheet bend.

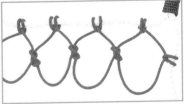

4 Make a bight and tie a sheet bend to the bottom of the bight made in the first row. Continue making bights (using the straight edge to guide you) and tie sheet bends to the bights made in the first row.

TYPE OF KNOT

LASHING

USE

DECORATIVE

OTHER NAMES

NONE

Most of us can plait three strands to make a braid in our hair. This four-strand sennit is also very easy to make. Four different-coloured lengths of thin cord produce this attractive rounded plait.

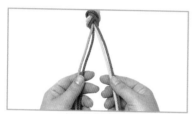

1 Take four strands of cord and bind them at one end. Now divide them into a left-hand and a right-hand pair.

2 First pass the outer strand of the right-hand pair of strands behind the other strands. Then bring it up between the two left-hand strands. Finally, place it so that it is lying next to its original companion.

3 Now take the outer strand of the left-hand pair behind the other strands so that it emerges between the two right-hand strands. Then bring it over to lie next to its original companion.

4 Repeat steps 2 and 3 until the required length is achieved, then bind the ends together. Make sure that you keep an even tension as the work progresses in length.

Jury mast knot

In nautical terms, 'jury' means 'makeshift' or 'temporary' and this flat knot was used to rig makeshift masts. Its attractive appearance makes it ideal for decorative use. Use brightly coloured, or gold, cord to make the knots, then stitch them to scatter cushions. Attached to a breast pocket, it could give a plain jacket a nautical makeover!

TYPE OF KNOT

LOOP

USE

DECORATIVE

OTHER NAMES

PITCHER KNOT

1 Make three large, loose, crossing turns by passing the rope behind itself. Each turn should overlap the previous one.

2 Inside the middle loop, further overlap the left-hand and right-hand loops. Make sure that you move the right over the left.

3 Find the middle loop's strands. Make a long left-hand loop by bringing the left-hand strand to the left, going under and over the two adjacent strands.

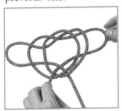

4 Make a long right-hand loop by taking the right-hand strand of the middle loop to the right. First go over, and then under, the two adjacent strands.

5 To make a third, upper loop, first find the upper edge of the centre loop and carefully pull it up. Form a symmetrical knot by adjusting the size of each of the three loops.

Index

Index

Bibliography

Ashley, C W, *The Ashley Book of Knots*, Garden City, NY, 1944.

Berthier, M P G, *The Art of Knots*, Garden City, NY, 1977.

Bigon, M, and Regazzoni, G, *The Morrow Guide to Knots*, NY, 1982.

Costantino, M, *The Knot Handbook*, Devon, England, 2000.

Gibson Fells, W B, *Official Guide to Knots and How to Tie Them*, NY, 1961.

Graumont, R, *Handbook of Knots*, London, 1977.

Kreh, L, and Sosin, M, *Practical Fishing and Boating Knots*, London, 1975.

March, B, *Rope Techniques in Mountaineering*, Cumbria, 1985.

Owen, P, *The Royal Yachting Association Book of Knots*, London, 2001.